EQUATIONS, INEQUALITIES, & VICs

Math Strategy Guide

This essential guide covers algebra in all its various forms (and disguises) on the GMAT. Master fundamental techniques and nuanced strategies to help you solve for unknown variables of every type.

Equations, Inequalities, and VICs GMAT Strategy Guide, Fourth Edition

10-digit International Standard Book Number: 0-9824238-1-0
13-digit International Standard Book Number: 978-0-9824238-1-3

Note: *GMAT, Graduate Management Admission Test, Graduate Management Admission Council,* and *GMAC* are all registered trademarks of the Graduate Management Admission Council which neither sponsors nor is affiliated in any way with this product.

8 GUIDE INSTRUCTIONAL SERIES

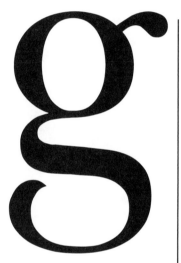

Math GMAT Strategy Guides

Number Properties (ISBN: 978-0-9824238-4-4)

Fractions, Decimals, & Percents (ISBN: 978-0-9824238-2-0)

Equations, Inequalities, & VICs (ISBN: 978-0-9824238-1-3)

Word Translations (ISBN: 978-0-9824238-7-5)

Geometry (ISBN: 978-0-9824238-3-7)

Verbal GMAT Strategy Guides

Critical Reasoning (ISBN: 978-0-9824238-0-6)

Reading Comprehension (ISBN: 978-0-9824238-5-1)

Sentence Correction (ISBN: 978-0-9824238-6-8)

ManhattanGMAT
the new standard

July 1st, 2010

Dear Student,

Thank you for picking up one of the Manhattan GMAT Strategy Guides—we hope that it refreshes your memory of the junior-high math that you haven't used in years. Maybe it will even teach you a new thing or two.

As with most accomplishments, there were many people involved in the various iterations of the book that you're holding. First and foremost is Zeke Vanderhoek, the founder of Manhattan GMAT. Zeke was a lone tutor in New York when he started the Company in 2000. Now, nine years later, MGMAT has Instructors and offices nationwide, and the Company contributes to the studies and successes of thousands of students each year.

Our 4th Edition Strategy Guides are based on the continuing experiences of our Instructors and our students. We owe much of these latest editions to the insight provided by our students. On the Company side, we are indebted to many of our Instructors, including but not limited to Josh Braslow, Dan Gonzalez, Mike Kim, Stacey Koprince, Ben Ku, Jadran Lee, David Mahler, Ron Purewal, Tate Shafer, Emily Sledge, and of course Chris Ryan, the Company's Lead Instructor and Director of Curriculum Development.

At Manhattan GMAT, we continually aspire to provide the best Instructors and resources possible. We hope that you'll find our dedication manifest in this book. If you have any comments or questions, please e-mail me at andrew.yang@manhattangmat.com. I'll be sure that your comments reach Chris and the rest of the team—and I'll read them too.

Best of luck in preparing for the GMAT!

Sincerely,

Andrew Yang
President
Manhattan GMAT

HOW TO ACCESS YOUR ONLINE RESOURCES

If you...

⊙ **are a registered Manhattan GMAT student**

and have received this book as part of your course materials, you have AUTOMATIC access to ALL of our online resources. This includes all practice exams, question banks, and online updates to this book. To access these resources, follow the instructions in the Welcome Guide provided to you at the start of your program. Do NOT follow the instructions below.

⊙ **purchased this book from the Manhattan GMAT Online store or at one of our Centers**

1. Go to: http://www.manhattangmat.com/practicecenter.cfm

2. Log in using the username and password used when your account was set up.

⊙ **purchased this book at a retail location**

1. Create an account with Manhattan GMAT at the website: https://www.manhattangmat.com/createaccount.cfm

2. Go to: http://www.manhattangmat.com/access.cfm

3. Follow the instructions on the screen.

Your one year of online access begins on the day that you register your book at the above URL.

You only need to register your product ONCE at the above URL. To use your online resources any time AFTER you have completed the registration process, login to the following URL: http://www.manhattangmat.com/practicecenter.cfm

Please note that online access is non-transferable. This means that only NEW and UNREGISTERED copies of the book will grant you online access. Previously used books will not provide any online resources.

⊙ **purchased an e-book version of this book**

1. Create an account with Manhattan GMAT at the website: https://www.manhattangmat.com/createaccount.cfm

2. Email a copy of your purchase receipt to books@manhattangmat.com to activate your resources. Please be sure to use the same email address to create an account that you used to purchase the e-book.

For any technical issues, email books@manhattangmat.com or call 800-576-4628.

Please refer to the following page for a description of the online resources that come with this book.

YOUR ONLINE RESOURCES

Your purchase includes ONLINE ACCESS to the following:

➤ 6 Computer Adaptive Online Practice Exams

The 6 full-length computer adaptive practice exams included with the purchase of this book are delivered online using Manhattan GMAT's proprietary computer-adaptive test engine. The exams adapt to your ability level by drawing from a bank of more than 1,200 unique questions of varying difficulty levels written by Manhattan GMAT's expert instructors, all of whom have scored in the 99th percentile on the Official GMAT. At the end of each exam you will receive a score, an analysis of your results, and the opportunity to review detailed explanations for each question. You may choose to take the exams timed or untimed.

The content presented in this book is updated periodically to ensure that it reflects the GMAT's most current trends and is as accurate as possible. You may view any known errors or minor changes upon registering for online access.

Important Note: The 6 computer adaptive online exams included with the purchase of this book are the SAME exams that you receive upon purchasing ANY book in Manhattan GMAT's 8 Book Strategy Series.

➤ *Equations, Inequalities, & VICs* Online Question Bank

The Bonus Online Question Bank for *Equations, Inequalities, & VICs* consists of 25 extra practice questions (with detailed explanations) that test the variety of concepts and skills covered in this book. These questions provide you with extra practice beyond the problem sets contained in this book. You may use our online timer to practice your pacing by setting time limits for each question in the bank.

➤ Online Updates to the Contents in this Book

The content presented in this book is updated periodically to ensure that it reflects the GMAT's most current trends. You may view all updates, including any known errors or changes, upon registering for online access.

PART I:
GENERAL

TABLE OF CONTENTS

PART II:
ADVANCED

TABLE OF CONTENTS

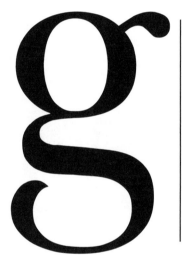

Chapter 1

of

EQUATIONS, INEQUALITIES, & VICs

BASIC EQUATIONS

In This Chapter . . .

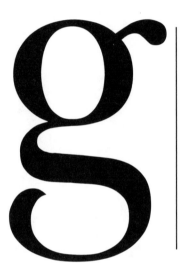

- Solving One-Variable Equations
- Simultaneous Equations: Solving by Substitution
- Simultaneous Equations: Solving by Combination
- Simultaneous Equations: Three Equations
- Mismatch Problems
- Combo Problems: Manipulations
- Testing Combos in Data Sufficiency
- Absolute Value Equations

BASIC EQUATIONS

Algebra is one of the major math topics tested on the GMAT. Your ability to solve equations is an essential component of your success on the exam.

Basic GMAT equations are those that DO NOT involve exponents. The GMAT expects you to solve several different types of BASIC equations :

1) An equation with 1 variable
2) Simultaneous equations with 2 or 3 variables
3) Mismatch equations
4) Combos
5) Equations with absolute value

Several of the preceding basic equation types probably look familiar to you. Others—particularly Mismatch Equations and Combos—are unique GMAT favorites that run counter to some of the rules you may have learned in high-school algebra. Becoming attuned to the particular subtleties of GMAT equations can be the difference between an average score and an excellent one.

Solving One-Variable Equations

Equations with one variable should be familiar to you from previous encounters with algebra. In order to solve one-variable equations, simply isolate the variable on one side of the equation. In doing so, make sure you perform identical operations to both sides of the equation. Here are three examples:

$$3x + 5 = 26$$ Subtract 5 from both sides.
$$3x = 21$$ Divide both sides by 3.
$$x = 7$$ 7 is the **solution** of the given equation.

$$w = 17w - 1$$ Subtract w from both sides.
$$0 = 16w - 1$$ Add 1 to both sides.
$$1 = 16w$$ Divide both sides by 16.
$$\frac{1}{16} = w$$

$$\frac{p}{9} + 3 = 5$$ Subtract 3 from both sides.

$$\frac{p}{9} = 2$$ Multiply both sides by 9.

$$p = 18$$

To solve basic equations, remember that whatever you do to one side, you must also do to the other side.

Simultaneous Equations: Solving by Substitution

Sometimes the GMAT asks you to solve a system of equations with more than one variable. You might be given two equations with two variables, or perhaps three equations with three variables. In either case, there are two primary ways of solving simultaneous equations: by substitution or by combination.

Solve the following for x and y.

$$x + y = 9$$
$$2x = 5y + 4$$

1. Solve the first equation for x. At this point, you will not get a number, of course.

$$x + y = 9$$
$$x = 9 - y$$

2. Substitute this expression involving y into the second equation wherever x appears.

$$2x = 5y + 4$$
$$2(9 - y) = 5y + 4$$

3. Solve the second equation for y. You will now get a number for y.

$$2(9 - y) = 5y + 4$$
$$18 - 2y = 5y + 4$$
$$14 = 7y$$
$$2 = y$$

4. Substitute your solution for y into the first equation in order to solve for x.

$$x + y = 9$$
$$x + 2 = 9$$
$$x = 7$$

Use substitution whenever one variable can be easily expressed in terms of the other.

Simultaneous Equations: Solving by Combination

Alternatively, you can solve simultaneous equations by combination. In this method, add or subtract the two equations to eliminate one of the variables.

>   Solve the following for x and y.

$$x + y = 9$$
$$2x = 5y + 4$$

1. Line up the terms of the equations.

$$x + y = 9$$
$$2x - 5y = 4$$

2. If you plan to add the equations, multiply one or both of the equations so that the coefficient of a variable in one equation is the OPPOSITE of that variable's coefficient in the other equation. If you plan to subtract them, multiply one or both of the equations so that the coefficient of a variable in one equation is the SAME as that variable's coefficient in the other equation.

$$-2(x + y = 9) \quad \rightarrow \quad -2x - 2y = -18$$
$$2x - 5y = 4 \quad \rightarrow \quad 2x - 5y = 4$$

Note that the x coefficients are now opposites.

3. Add the equations to eliminate one of the variables.

$$\begin{array}{r} -2x - 2y = -18 \\ +\ \ 2x - 5y = \ \ \ 4 \\ \hline -7y = -14 \end{array}$$

4. Solve the resulting equation for the unknown variable.

$$-7y = -14$$
$$y = 2$$

5. Substitute into one of the original equations to solve for the second variable.

$$x + y = 9$$
$$x + 2 = 9$$
$$x = 7$$

Use combination whenever it is easy to manipulate the equations so that the coefficients for one variable are the SAME or OPPOSITE.

Simultaneous Equations: Three Equations

The procedure for solving a system of three equations with three variables is exactly the same as for a system with two equations and two variables. You can use substitution or combination. This example uses both:

Solve the following for *w*, *x*, and *y*.

$$x + w = y$$
$$2y + w = 3x - 2$$
$$13 - 2w = x + y$$

1. The first equation is already solved for *y*.

$$y = x + w$$

2. Substitute for *y* in the second and third equations.

Substitute for *y* in the second equation:
$$2(x + w) + w = 3x - 2$$
$$2x + 2w + w = 3x - 2$$
$$-x + 3w = -2$$

Substitute for *y* in the third equation:
$$13 - 2w = x + (x + w)$$
$$13 - 2w = 2x + w$$
$$3w + 2x = 13$$

3. Multiply the first of the resulting two-variable equations by (−1) and combine them with addition.

$$\begin{array}{r} x - 3w = 2 \\ + \ \underline{2x + 3w = 13} \\ 3x = 15 \end{array}$$

Therefore, *x* = 5

4. Use your solution for *x* to determine solutions for the other two variables.

$$3w + 2x = 13$$
$$3w + 10 = 13$$
$$3w = 3$$
$$w = 1$$

$$y = x + w$$
$$y = 5 + 1$$
$$y = 6$$

The preceding example requires a lot of steps to solve. Therefore, it is unlikely that the GMAT will ask you to solve such a complex system—it would be difficult to complete in two minutes. Here is the key to handling systems of three or more equations on the GMAT: look for ways to simplify the work. Look especially for shortcuts or symmetries in the form of the equations to reduce the number of steps needed to solve the system.

Take this system as an example:

What is the sum of x, y and z?

$$x + y = 8$$
$$x + z = 11$$
$$y + z = 7$$

In this case, DO NOT try to solve for x, y, and z individually. Instead, notice the symmetry of the equations—each one adds exactly two of the variables—and add them all together:

$$
\begin{array}{r}
x + y \quad\;\; = \;\; 8 \\
x \quad\;\; + z = 11 \\
+ \quad\; + y + z = \;\; 7 \\
\hline
2x + 2y + 2z = 26
\end{array}
$$

Therefore, $x + y + z$ is half of 26, or 13.

Do not assume that the number of equations must be equal to the number of variables.

Mismatch Problems

Consider the following rule, which you might have learned in a basic algebra course: if you are trying to solve for 2 different variables, you need 2 equations. If you are trying to solve for 3 different variables, you need 3 equations, etc. The GMAT loves to trick you by taking advantage of your faith in this easily misapplied rule.

MISMATCH problems, which are particularly common on the Data Sufficiency portion of the test, are those in which the number of unknown variables does NOT correspond to the number of given equations. Do not try to apply that old rule you learned in high-school algebra. All MISMATCH problems must be solved on a case-by-case basis. Try the following Data Sufficiency problem:

What is x?

(1) $\dfrac{3x}{3y + 5z} = 8$ (2) $6y + 10z = 18$

It is tempting to say that these two equations are not sufficient to solve for x, since there are 3 variables and only 2 equations. However, the question does NOT ask you to solve for all three variables. It only asks you to solve for x, which IS possible:

First, get the x term on one side of the equation:

Then, notice that the second equation gives us a value for $3y + 5z$, which we can substitute into the first equation in order to solve for x:

$$\frac{3x}{3y + 5z} = 8$$

$$3x = 8(3y + 5z)$$

$6y + 10z = 18$	$3x = 8(3y + 5z)$
$2(3y + 5z) = 18$	$3x = 8(9)$
$3y + 5z = 9$	$x = 8(3) = 24$

The answer is **(C)**: BOTH statements TOGETHER are sufficient.

Now consider an example in which 2 equations with 2 unknowns are actually NOT sufficient to solve a problem:

What is x?

(1) $y = x^3 - 1$ (2) $y = x - 1$

It is tempting to say that these 2 equations are surely sufficient to solve for x, since there are 2 different equations and only 2 variables. However, notice that if we take the expression for y in the first equation and substitute into the second, we actually get multiple possibilities for x. (In Chapter 3, we will learn more about how to solve these sorts of equations.)

Follow through with the algebra on potential mismatch problems to determine whether a single solution is possible.

$$x^3 - 1 = x - 1 \qquad\qquad x(x^2 - 1) = 0$$

$$x^3 = x \qquad\qquad x(x+1)(x-1) = 0$$

$$x^3 - x = 0 \qquad\qquad x = \{-1, 0, 1\}$$

Because of the exponent (3) on x, it turns out that we have THREE possible values for x. If x equals either -1, 0, or 1, then the equation $x^3 = x$ will be true. We can say that this equation has *three solutions* or *three roots*. Therefore, we cannot find a single value for x. The answer to the problem is **(E)**: the statements together are NOT sufficient.

Now consider another example in which 2 equations with 2 unknowns are actually NOT sufficient to solve a problem. This time, it looks as if we are avoiding exponents altogether:

What is x?

(1) $x - y = 1$ (2) $xy = 12$

Again, it is tempting to say that these 2 equations are sufficient to solve for x, since there are 2 equations and only 2 variables. However, when you actually combine the two equations, you wind up with a so-called "quadratic" equation. An exponent of 2 appears naturally in the algebra below, and we wind up with two solutions or roots. (Again, we will cover the specific solution process for quadratic equations in Chapter 3.)

$$x - y = 1$$
$$x - 1 = y$$
$$x(x-1) = 12$$
$$x^2 - x = 12$$
$$x^2 - x - 12 = 0$$
$$(x-4)(x+3) = 0$$
$$x = 4 \ \text{ or } \ x = -3$$

The combined equation has two solutions or roots. Although we have narrowed down the possibilities for x to just two choices, we do NOT have sufficient information to solve uniquely for x. Again, the answer is **(E)**: the statements together are NOT sufficient.

A MASTER RULE for determining whether 2 equations involving 2 variables (say, x and y) will be sufficient to solve for the variables is this:

(1) If both of the equations are linear—that is, if there are no squared terms (such as x^2 or y^2) and no xy terms—the equations will be sufficient UNLESS the two equations are mathematically identical (e.g., $x + y = 10$ is identical to $2x + 2y = 20$).

(2) If there are ANY non-linear terms in either of the equations (such as x^2, y^2, xy, or $\dfrac{x}{y}$), there will USUALLY be two (or more) different solutions for each of the variables and the equations will not be sufficient.

Examples:

What is x?

   (1) $2x + 3y = 8$
   (2) $2x - y = 0$

Because both of the equations are linear, and because they are not mathematically identical, there is only one solution ($x = 1$ and $y = 2$) so the statements are SUFFICIENT TOGETHER (answer **C**).

What is x?

   (1) $x^2 + y = 17$
   (2) $y = 2x + 2$

Because there is an x^2 term in equation 1, as usual there are two solutions for x and y ($x = 3$ and $y = 8$, or $x = -5$ and $y = -8$), so the statements are NOT SUFFICIENT, even together (answer **E**).

> With 2 equations and 2 unknowns, linear equations usually lead to one solution, and nonlinear equations usually lead to 2 (or more) solutions.

Combo Problems: Manipulations

The GMAT often asks you to solve for a combination of variables, called COMBO problems. For example, a question might ask, what is the value of $x + y$?

In these cases, since you are not asked to solve for one specific variable, you should generally NOT try to solve for the individual variables right away. Instead, you should try to manipulate the given equation(s) so that the COMBO is isolated on one side of the equation. Only try to solve for the individual variables after you have exhausted all other avenues.

There are four easy manipulations that are the key to solving most COMBO problems. You can use the acronym **MADS** to remember them.

M: Multiply or divide the whole equation by a certain number.
A: Add or subtract a number on both sides of the equation.
D: Distribute or factor an expression on ONE side of the equation.
S: Square or unsquare both sides of the equation.

Here are three examples, each of which uses one or more of these manipulations:

If $x = \dfrac{7-y}{2}$, what is $2x + y$?

$$x = \dfrac{7-y}{2}$$
$$2x = 7 - y$$
$$2x + y = 7$$

Here, getting rid of the denominator by multiplying both sides of the equation by 2 is the key to isolating the combo on one side of the equation.

If $\sqrt{2t+r} = 5$, what is $3r + 6t$?

$$\left(\sqrt{2t+r}\right)^2 = 5^2$$
$$2t + r = 25$$
$$6t + 3r = 75$$

Here, getting rid of the square root by squaring both sides of the equation is the first step. Then, multiplying the whole equation by 3 forms the combo in question.

If $a(4 - c) = 2ac + 4a + 9$, what is ac?

$$4a - ac = 2ac + 4a + 9$$
$$-ac = 2ac + 9$$
$$-3ac = 9$$
$$ac = -3$$

Here, distributing the term on the left-hand side of the equation is the first key to isolating the combo on one side of the equation; then we have to subtract $2ac$ from both sides of the equation.

Testing Combos in Data Sufficiency

Combo problems occur most frequently in Data Sufficiency. Whenever you detect that a Data Sufficiency question may involve a combo, you should try to manipulate the given equation(s) in either the question or the statement, so that the combo is isolated on one side of the equation. Then, if the other side of an equation from a statement contains a VALUE, that equation is SUFFICIENT. If the other side of the equation contains a VARIABLE EXPRESSION, that equation is NOT SUFFICIENT.

What is $\dfrac{\frac{2}{y}}{\frac{4}{x}}$?

(1) $\dfrac{x+y}{y} = 3$

(2) $x + y = 12$

Avoid attempting to solve for the individual variables in a combo problem, unless there is no obvious alternative.

First, rephrase the question by manipulating the given expression:

$$\frac{\frac{2}{y}}{\frac{4}{x}} = ? \qquad \frac{2}{y} \times \frac{x}{4} = \frac{2x}{4y} = \frac{x}{2y} = \frac{1}{2} \times \frac{x}{y} = ?$$

Now, we can ignore the 1/2 and isolate the combo we are looking for:

$\dfrac{x}{y} = ?$ We are looking for the ratio of x to y.

Manipulate statement (1) to solve for $\dfrac{x}{y}$ on one side of the equation. Since the other side of the equation contains a VALUE, statement (1) is SUFFICIENT:

$$\frac{x+y}{y} = 3 \qquad\qquad x = 2y$$

$$x + y = 3y \qquad\qquad \frac{x}{y} = 2$$

Manipulate statement (2) to solve for $\dfrac{x}{y}$ on one side of the equation. Since the other side of the equation contains a VARIABLE EXPRESSION, Statement (2) is INSUFFICIENT:

$$x + y = 12 \qquad\qquad \frac{x}{y} = \frac{12 - y}{y}$$

$$x = 12 - y \qquad\qquad \frac{x}{y} = \frac{12}{y} - 1$$

The key to solving this problem easily is to AVOID trying to solve for the individual variables.

Absolute Value Equations

Absolute value refers to the POSITIVE value of the expression within the absolute value brackets. Equations that involve absolute value generally have TWO SOLUTIONS. In other words, there are TWO numbers that the variable could equal in order to make the equation true. The reason is that the value of the expression *inside* the absolute value brackets could be POSITIVE OR NEGATIVE. For instance, if we know $|x| = 5$, then x could be either 5 or -5, and the equation would still be true.

It is important to consider this rule when thinking about GMAT questions that involve absolute value. The following three-step method should be used when solving for a variable expression inside absolute value brackets. Consider this example:

Do not forget to check each of your solutions to absolute value equations by putting each solution back into the original equation.

Solve for w, given that $12 + |w - 4| = 30$.

Step 1. Isolate the expression within the absolute value brackets.

$$12 + |w - 4| = 30$$
$$|w - 4| = 18$$

Step 2. Once we have an equation of the form $|x| = a$ with $a > 0$, we know that $x = \pm a$.

Remove the absolute value brackets and solve the equation for 2 different cases:

<u>CASE 1: $x = a$ (x is positive)</u>

$$w - 4 = 18$$
$$w = 22$$

<u>CASE 2: $x = -a$ (x is negative)</u>

$$w - 4 = -18$$
$$w = -14$$

Step 3. Check to see whether each solution is valid by putting each one back into the original equation and verifying that the two sides of the equation are in fact equal.

In case 1, the solution, $w = 22$, is valid because $12 + |22 - 4| = 12 + 18 = 30$.
In case 2, the solution, $w = -14$, is valid because $12 + |-14 - 4| = 12 + 18 = 30$.

Consider another example:
Solve for n, given that $|n + 9| - 3n = 3$.

Again, isolate the expression within the absolute value brackets and consider both cases.

1. $|n + 9| = 3 + 3n$

2.   <u>CASE 1: $n + 9$ is positive:</u>

$$n + 9 = 3 + 3n$$
$$n = 3$$

<u>CASE 2: $n + 9$ is negative:</u>

$$n + 9 = -(3 + 3n)$$
$$n = -3$$

3. The first solution, $n = 3$, is valid because $|(3) + 9| - 3(3) = 12 - 9 = 3$.

However, the second solution, $n = -3$, is NOT valid, since $|(-3) + 9| - 3(-3) = 6 + 9 = 15$. This solution fails because when $n = -3$, the absolute value expression ($n + 9 = 6$) is not negative, even though we assumed it was negative when we calculated that solution.

The possibility of a failed solution is a peculiarity of absolute value equations. For most other types of equations, it is good to check your solutions, but doing so is less critical.

Problem Set

For problems #1–5, solve for all unknowns.

1. $\dfrac{3x - 6}{5} = x - 6$

2. $\dfrac{x + 2}{4 + x} = \dfrac{5}{9}$

3. $22 - \left| y + 14 \right| = 20$

4. $y = 2x + 9$ and $7x + 3y = -51$

5. $a + b = 10$, $b + c = 12$, and $a + c = 16$

For problems #6–8, determine whether it is *possible* to solve for x using the given equations. (Do not solve.)

6. $\dfrac{\sqrt{x}}{6a} = T$ and $\dfrac{Ta}{4} = 14$

7. $3x + 2a = 8$ and $6a = 24 - 9x$

8. $3a + 2b + x = 8$ and $12a + 8b + 2x = 4$

For problems #9–12, solve for the specified expression.

9.   Given that $\dfrac{x + y}{3} = 17$, what is $x + y$?

10.   Given that $\dfrac{a + b}{b} = 21$, what is $\dfrac{a}{b}$?

11.   Given that $10x + 10y = x + y + 81$, what is $x + y$?

12.   Given that $\dfrac{b + a}{2a} = 2$ and $a + b = 8$, what is a?

For #13–15, write the expression in factored form (if distributed) and in distributed form (if factored):

13. $y^6 - y^4$

14. $5^6 - 5^5 + 5^4$

15. $(q + r)(s + t)$

1. $x = 12$:

$$\frac{3x - 6}{5} = x - 6$$
$$3x - 6 = 5(x - 6)$$
$$3x - 6 = 5x - 30$$
$$24 = 2x$$
$$12 = x$$

Solve by multiplying both sides by 5 to eliminate the denominator. Then, distribute and isolate the variable on the left side.

2. $x = \frac{1}{2}$:

$$\frac{x + 2}{4 + x} = \frac{5}{9}$$
$$9(x + 2) = 5(4 + x)$$
$$9x + 18 = 20 + 5x$$
$$4x = 2$$
$$x = \frac{1}{2}$$

Cross-multiply to eliminate the denominators. Then, distribute and solve.

3. $y = \{-16, -12\}$:

$$22 - |y + 14| = 20$$
$$|y + 14| = 2$$

First, isolate the expression within the absolute value brackets. Then, solve for two cases, one in which the expression is positive and one in which it is negative. Finally, test the validity of your solutions.

Case 1: $y + 14 = 2$ Case 2: $y + 14 = -2$
        $y = -12$ $y = -16$

Case 1 is valid because $22 - |-12 + 14| = 22 - 2 = 20$.
Case 2 is valid because $22 - |-16 + 14| = 22 - 2 = 20$.

4. $x = -6$; $y = -3$:

$$y = 2x + 9 \qquad 7x + 3y = -51$$
$$7x + 3(2x + 9) = -51$$
$$7x + 6x + 27 = -51$$
$$13x + 27 = -51$$
$$13x = -78$$
$$x = -6$$

$$y = 2x + 9 = 2(-6) + 9 = -3$$

Solve this system by substitution. Substitute the value given for y in the first equation into the second equation. Then, distribute, combine like terms, and solve. Once you get a value for x, substitute it back into the first equation to obtain the value of y.

5. $a = 7$; $b = 3$; $c = 9$: This problem could be solved by an elaborate series of substitutions. However, because the coefficients on each variable in each equation are equal to 1, combination proves easier. Here is one way, though certainly not the only way, to solve the problem:

$$\begin{array}{r} a + b = 10 \\ b + c = 12 \\ \hline a + c = 16 \\ \hline 2a + 2b + 2c = 38 \end{array}$$

First, combine all three equations by adding them together. Then divide by 2 to get the sum of all three equations. Subtracting any of the original equations from this new equation will solve for one of the variables, and the rest can be solved by plugging back into the original equations.

$$\begin{array}{r} a + b + c = 19 \\ -(a + b = 10) \\ \hline c = 9 \end{array}$$

$$b + 9 = 12 \qquad a + 9 = 16$$
$$b = 3 \qquad a = 7$$

6. **YES:** This problem contains 3 variables and 2 equations. However, this is not enough to conclude that you cannot solve for x. You must check to see if you can solve by isolating a combination of variables, as shown below:

$$\frac{\sqrt{x}}{6a} = T \text{ and } \frac{Ta}{4} = 14$$
$$x = (6Ta)^2 \text{ and } Ta = 56$$
$$x = (6 \times 56)^2$$

We can find a value for x.

7. **NO:** This problem contains 2 variables and 2 equations. However, this is not enough to conclude that you can solve for x. If one equation is merely a multiple of the other one, then you will not have a unique solution for x. In this case, the second equation is merely 3 times the first, so the equations cannot be combined to find the value of x:

$$6a = 24 - 9x$$
$$9x + 6a = 24$$
$$3x + 2a = 8$$

8. **YES:** This problem contains 3 variables and 2 equations. However, this is not enough to conclude that you cannot solve for x. You must check to see if you can solve by eliminating all the variables but x, as shown below:

$$(4)[3a + 2b + x = 8] \qquad \rightarrow \qquad \begin{array}{r} 12a + 8b + 4x = 32 \\ - 12a + 8b + 2x = 4 \\ \hline 2x = 28 \\ x = 14 \end{array}$$

9. $x + y = 51$:

$$\frac{x + y}{3} = 17$$
$$x + y = 51$$

*Manhattan*GMAT Prep
the new standard

10. $\dfrac{a}{b} = 20$:

$$\frac{a+b}{b} = 21$$

$$\frac{a}{b} + 1 = 21$$

$$\frac{a}{b} = 20$$

11. $x + y = 9$:

$$10x + 10y = x + y + 81$$
$$9x + 9y = 81$$
$$x + y = 9$$

12. $a = 2$:

$$\frac{\dfrac{b+a}{2a} = 2}{a+b = 8}$$

$$\frac{1}{2a} = \frac{1}{4}$$

$$\frac{b+a}{2a(a+b)} = \frac{2}{8}$$

$$a = 2$$

We can divide the first equation by the second equation to solve for a quickly.

Alternatively, we could substitute for $b + a$ in the first equation, using the second.

13. $y^6 - y^4 = y^4(y^2 - 1) = \boldsymbol{y^4(y+1)(y-1)}$

14. $5^6 - 5^5 + 5^4 = 5^4(5^2 - 5^1 + 1) = 5^4(25 - 5 + 1) = \boldsymbol{21 \cdot 5^4}$

15. $(q+r)(s+t) = \boldsymbol{qs + qt + rs + rt}$

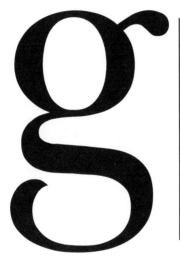

Chapter 2
of

EQUATIONS, INEQUALITIES, & VICs

EQUATIONS
WITH EXPONENTS

In This Chapter . . .

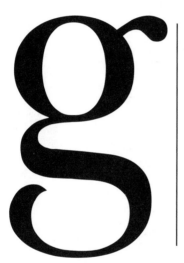

- Even Exponent Equations: 2 Solutions
- Odd Exponents: 1 Solution
- Same Base or Same Exponent
- Eliminating Roots: Square Both Sides

EXPONENTIAL EQUATIONS

The GMAT tests more than your knowledge of basic equations. In fact, the GMAT often complicates equations by including exponents or roots with the unknown variables.

Equations with exponents take various forms. Here are some examples:

$$x^3 = -125 \qquad\qquad y^2 + 3 = x \qquad\qquad \sqrt{x} + 15 = 21$$

There are two keys to achieving success with equations that include:

1) Know the RULES for exponents and roots. You will recall that these rules were covered in the "Exponents" Chapter of the Manhattan GMAT *Number Properties* Strategy Guide. It is essential to know these rules by heart. In particular, you should review the rules for combining exponential expressions.

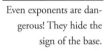

2) Remember that EVEN EXPONENTS are DANGEROUS because they hide the sign of the base. In general, equations with even exponents have 2 solutions.

Even Exponent Equations: 2 Solutions

Recall from the rules of exponents that **even exponents are dangerous** in the hands of the GMAT test writers.

Why are they dangerous? Even exponents hide the sign of the base. As a result, equations involving variables with even exponents can have both a positive and a negative solution. This should remind you of absolute values. Compare these two equations:

$$x^2 = 25 \qquad\qquad |x| = 5$$

Do you see what they have in common? In both cases, $x = \pm 5$. The equations share the same two solutions. In fact, there is an important relationship: **for any x, $\sqrt{x^2} = |x|$.**

Here is another example:

$a^2 - 5 = 12$ By adding 5 to both sides, we can rewrite this equation as $a^2 = 17$. This equation has two solutions: $\sqrt{17}$ and $-\sqrt{17}$.

As we saw in Chapter 1, we can also say that the equation $a^2 = 17$ has two *roots*. Notice that the roots or solutions of an equation do not literally have to be square roots, though!

Also note that not all equations with even exponents have 2 solutions. For example:

$x^2 + 3 = 3$ By subtracting 3 from both sides, we can rewrite this equation as $x^2 = 0$, which has only one solution: 0.

$x^2 + 9 = 0$??   Squaring can never produce a negative number!
$x^2 = -9$??   This equation does not have any solutions.

Odd Exponents: 1 Solution

Equations that involve only odd exponents or cube roots have only 1 solution:

$x^3 = -125$ Here, x has only 1 solution: -5. You can see that $(-5)(-5)(-5) = -125$. This will not work with positive 5.

$243 = y^5$ Here, y has only 1 solution: 3. You can see that $(3)(3)(3)(3)(3) = 243$. This will not work with negative 3.

If an equation includes some variables with odd exponents and some variables with even exponents, treat it as dangerous, as it is likely to have 2 solutions. Any even exponents in an equation make it dangerous.

Rewrite exponential equations so they have either the same base or the same exponent.

Same Base or Same Exponent

In problems that involve exponential expressions on BOTH sides of the equation, it is imperative to REWRITE the bases so that either the same base or the same exponent appears on both sides of the exponential equation. Once you do this, you can usually eliminate the bases or the exponents and rewrite the remainder as an equation.

Solve the following equation for w: $(4^w)^3 = 32^{w-1}$

1. Rewrite the bases so that the same base appears on both sides of the equation. Right now, the left side has a base of 4 and the right side has a base of 32. Notice that both 4 and 32 can be expressed as powers of 2. So we can rewrite 4 as 2^2, and we can rewrite 32 as 2^5.

2. Plug the rewritten bases into the original equation.
$$(4^w)^3 = 32^{w-1}$$
$$((2^2)^w)^3 = (2^5)^{w-1}$$

3. Simplify the equation using the rules of exponents.
$$((2^2)^w)^3 = (2^5)^{w-1}$$
$$2^{6w} = 2^{5(w-1)}$$

4. Eliminate the identical bases, rewrite the exponents as an equation, and solve.
$$6w = 5w - 5$$
$$w = -5$$

You must be careful if 0, 1, or -1 is the base (or could be the base), since the outcome of raising those bases to powers is not unique. For instance, $0^2 = 0^3 = 0^{29} = 0$. So if $0^x = 0^y$, we cannot claim that $x = y$. Likewise, $1^2 = 1^3 = 1^{29} = 1$, and $(-1)^2 = (-1)^4 = (-1)^{even} = 1$, while $(-1)^3 = (-1)^5 = (-1)^{odd} = -1$. Fortunately, the GMAT rarely tries to trick us this way.

*Manhattan*GMAT*Prep
the new standard

Eliminating Roots: Square Both Sides

The most effective way to solve problems that involve variables underneath radical symbols (variable square roots) is to square both sides of the equation.

Solve the following equation for s: $\sqrt{s-12}=7$

$\sqrt{s-12}=7$ Squaring both sides of the equation eliminates the radical
$s-12=49$ symbol and allows us to solve for s more easily.
$s=61$

Given that $\sqrt{3b-8}=\sqrt{12-b}$, what is b?

$\sqrt{3b-8}=\sqrt{12-b}$
$3b-8=12-b$ Squaring both sides of the equation eliminates both radical
$4b-8=12$ symbols and allows us to solve for b more easily.
$4b=20$
$b=5$

Whenever you square an equation to solve it, be sure to check the solutions you get in the original equation.

After you have solved for the variable, check that the solution works in the original equation. Squaring both sides can actually introduce an extraneous solution. We saw a similar issue in absolute value equations in the previous chapter: you must check the solutions.

Solve the following equation for x: $\sqrt{x}=x-2$

$\sqrt{x}=x-2$
$x=(x-2)^2=x^2-4x+4$
$0=x^2-5x+4$
$0=(x-4)(x-1)$
$x=4 \text{ or } 1$

However, only 4 works in the original equation: $\sqrt{4}=4-2$ but $\sqrt{1}=1-2?$
                                                $2=2$ $1\neq-1$

Thus, the only possible value for x is 4.

Remember also that the written square root symbol only works over positive numbers (or zero) and only yields positive numbers (or zero). The square root of a negative number is not defined, and the GMAT does not test undefined or imaginary numbers.

$\sqrt{x}=5$ means $x=25$

At the same time, there are two numbers whose square is 25: that is, 5 and −5.

For equations that involve cube roots, solve by cubing both sides of the equation:

Solve the following equation for y: $-3 = \sqrt[3]{y-8}$

$$-3 = \sqrt[3]{y-8}$$ Cubing both sides of the equation eliminates the radical.
$$-27 = y - 8$$
$$-19 = y$$

Remember that cubing a number preserves the sign, so no extraneous solution can be introduced when you cube an equation.

Problem Set

1. Given that $\sqrt{t+8} = 6$, what is t?

2. Given that $\sqrt{m+4} = \sqrt{2m-11}$, what is m?

3. Given that $\sqrt{\sqrt{2x}+23} = 5$, what is x?

4. Given that $5 - \sqrt{y^2} = -3$, what is y?

5. Given that $\sqrt{x^2-2} - \sqrt{x} = 0$, what is x?

6. If u is a positive integer, which of the following could be a negative number?
   (A) $u^7 - u^6$ (B) $u^3 + u^4 + u^5$ (C) u^{-9} (D) $u^{-13} + u^{13}$ (E) $u^3 - u^8$

7. Simplify, given that $x \neq 0$: $\left(\dfrac{x^{21}}{x^3} \right)^7$

8. Given that $2x + y = -3$ and $x^2 = y + 3$, solve for x and y.

9. If $x^4 = 81$, $z^3 = -125$, and $d^2 = 4$, what is the smallest possible value of $x + z + d$?

10. Given that k and m are positive integers, $(x^4)(x^8) = (x^k)^m$ (with $x \neq 0, 1,$ or -1), and also $m = k + 1$, solve for k and m.

11. Given that $(3^k)^4 = 27$, what is k?

12. Given that $x + y = 13$ and $\sqrt{y} = x - 1$, solve for the *positive* values of x and y.

For problems #13–15, given that x is an integer greater than 1, determine whether each of the following expressions <u>can</u> be an integer.

13. $x^7 + x^{-7}$

14. $x^{\frac{1}{4}} + x^{\frac{1}{2}}$

15. $x^{\frac{1}{3}} + x^0 + x^5$

1. **28:**

$$\sqrt{t+8} = 6$$
$$t + 8 = 36$$
$$t = 28$$

Square both sides to eliminate the radical. Then, solve for t. You should check that the solution works in the original equation, but you can do so mentally with a simple equation such as this one.

2. **15:**

$$\sqrt{m+4} = \sqrt{2m-11}$$
$$m + 4 = 2m - 11$$
$$15 = m$$

Square both sides to eliminate the radicals. Then, solve for m. Again, check that the solution works in the original equation.

3. **$x = 2$:**

$$\sqrt{\sqrt{2x+23}} = 5$$
$$\sqrt{2x+23} = 25$$
$$\sqrt{2x} = 2$$
$$2x = 4$$
$$x = 2$$

Square both sides; this eliminates the larger radical sign on the left side of the equation. Then, subtract 23 from both sides to isolate the variable. Square both sides again to eliminate the radical. Finally, divide both sides by 2 to find the value of x. Check that the solution works in the original equation.

4. **$y = \{8, -8\}$:**

$$5 - \sqrt{y^2} = -3$$
$$5 + 3 = \sqrt{y^2}$$
$$64 = y^2$$
$$\{8, -8\} = y$$

Solve for $\sqrt{y^2}$ on one side of the equation first, then square both sides. Remember that since y^2 has an even exponent, y could be positive or negative. Both solutions work in the original equation, as you can easily check.

5. **$x = 2$ only:**

$$\sqrt{x^2-2} - \sqrt{x} = 0 \qquad\qquad x^2 - x - 2 = 0$$
$$\sqrt{x^2-2} = \sqrt{x} \qquad\qquad (x-2)(x+1) = 0$$
$$x^2 - 2 = x \qquad\qquad x = \{2, -1\}$$

Solve by moving $\sqrt{x}$ to the right-hand side of the equation first, then square both sides.

There seem to be two solutions: -1 and 2. However, -1 is not a viable solution because you cannot take the square root of negative numbers. That solution is an artifact of the squaring method, not an actual solution to the original equation.

6. **(E):** If u is a positive integer, $u^8 > u^3$. Therefore, $u^3 - u^8 < 0$.

7. **x^{126}:**

$$\left(\frac{x^{21}}{x^3}\right)^7 = (x^{21-3})^7 = (x^{18})^7 = x^{18\cdot7} = x^{126}$$

8. $x = 0, y = -3$ OR $x = -2, y = 1$ (**both solutions are possible**):

$$2x + y = -3 \qquad\qquad x^2 = y + 3$$
$$y = -2x - 3 \qquad\qquad y = x^2 - 3$$

$$-2x - 3 = x^2 - 3$$
$$x^2 + 2x = 0$$
$$x(x + 2) = 0$$

$$x = 0 \qquad \text{OR} \qquad x + 2 = 0$$
$$x = -2$$

Rearrange each equation so that it expresses y in terms of x. Then, set the right sides of both equations equal to each other and solve for x. Substitute each value of x into either equation to find the corresponding value for y.

If $x = 0$, then $y = x^2 - 3 = (0)^2 - 3 = -3$

If $x = -2$, then $y = x^2 - 3 = (-2)^2 - 3 = 1$

9. $-$**10**:

If $x^4 = 81$, $x = \{-3, 3\}$.
If $z^3 = -125$, $z = -5$.
If $d^2 = 4$, $d = \{-2, 2\}$.

To find the smallest possible value of $x + z + d$, select the smallest value for each variable:

$$x = -3 \qquad\qquad y = -5 \qquad\qquad z = -2$$

$$x + z + d = -10$$

10. $k = 3, m = 4$:

$$(x^4)(x^8) = (x^k)^m \text{ and } m = k + 1$$
$$x^{12} = x^{km}$$
$$km = 12$$
$$k(k + 1) = 12$$
$$k^2 + k = 12$$
$$k^2 + k - 12 = 0$$
$$(k - 3)(k + 4) = 0$$

$$k - 3 = 0 \qquad \text{OR} \qquad k + 4 = 0$$
$$k = 3 \qquad\qquad\qquad k = -4$$

Since x is not one of the "dangerous bases" (0, 1, or -1), we can drop the x.

Since we know that k and m are both positive integers, k must be equal to 3. Therefore, $m = k + 1 = 4$.

11. $k = \dfrac{3}{4}$:

$$(3^k)^4 = 27$$
$$3^{4k} = 3^3$$
$$4k = 3$$
$$k = \frac{3}{4}$$

12. $x = 4$, $y = 9$:

$x + y = 13$	$\sqrt{y} = x - 1$
$y = 13 - x$	$y = (x - 1)(x - 1)$
	$y = x^2 - 2x + 1$

$$13 - x = x^2 - 2x + 1$$
$$x^2 - x - 12 = 0$$
$$(x - 4)(x + 3) = 0$$

$$x - 4 = 0 \quad \text{OR} \quad x + 3 = 0$$
$$x = 4 \qquad\qquad x = -3$$

$$y = 13 - x = 13 - 4 = 9$$

Solve both equations for y in terms of x. Then, set the right side of each equation equal to each other. Solve the quadratic equation by factoring (see the next chapter if necessary). Since we are asked only for the positive values, discard –3. Then, substitute the remaining value for x (that is, 4) into either equation to find the corresponding value for y.

13. **NO:** The only value of x for which $x^7 + x^{-7} = x^7 + \dfrac{1}{x^7}$ can be an integer is 1.

If $x = 1$, then $x^7 + x^{-7} = 1^7 + 1^{-7} = 1 + 1 = 2$.

However, we know that x must be an integer greater than 1.

14. **YES:** If $x = 16$, $x^{\frac{1}{4}} + x^{\frac{1}{2}} = \sqrt[4]{16} + \sqrt{16} = 2 + 4 = 6$. If x is any number with an integer fourth root, this sum will be an integer.

15. **YES:** If $x = 8$, $x^{\frac{1}{3}} + x^0 + x^5 = \sqrt[3]{8} + 8^0 + 8^5 = 2 + 1 + 32{,}768 = 32{,}771$. If x is any perfect cube, this sum will be an integer. Of course, you don't have to figure out 8^5. Any integer raised to the power of a positive integer will be another integer: $8^5 = 8 \times 8 \times 8 \times 8 \times 8 =$ some big integer.

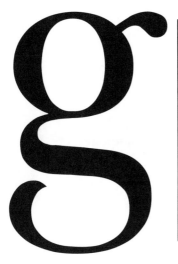

Chapter 3

of

EQUATIONS, INEQUALITIES, & VICs

QUADRATIC EQUATIONS

In This Chapter . . .

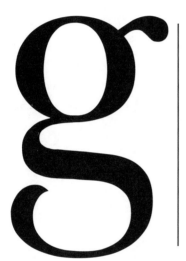

- Factoring Quadratic Equations
- Disguised Quadratics
- Going in Reverse: Use FOIL
- Using FOIL with Square Roots
- One-Solution Quadratics
- Zero in the Denominator: Undefined
- The Three Special Products

QUADRATIC EQUATIONS

One special type of even exponent equation is called the quadratic equation. Here are some examples of quadratic equations:

$$x^2 + 3x + 8 = 12 \qquad w^2 - 16w + 1 = 0 \qquad 2y^2 - y + 5 = 8$$

Quadratic equations are equations with one unknown and two defining components:
    (1) a variable term raised to the second power
    (2) a variable term raised to the first power

Here are other ways of writing quadratics:

$$x^2 = 3x + 4 \qquad a = 5a^2 \qquad 6 - b = 7b^2$$

Like other even exponent equations, quadratic equations generally have 2 solutions. That is, there are usually two possible values of x (or whatever the variable is) that make the equation <u>true</u>.

Factoring Quadratic Equations

The following example illustrates the process for solving quadratic equations:

    Given that $x^2 + 3x + 8 = 12$, what is x?

1.   Move all the terms to the left side of the equation, combine them, and put them in the form $ax^2 + bx + c$ (where a, b, and c are integers). The right side of the equation should be set to 0. (Usually, this process makes the x^2 term positive. If not, move all the terms to the right side of the equation instead.)

     $x^2 + 3x + 8 = 12$ Subtracting 12 from both sides of the equation puts all the
     $x^2 + 3x - 4 = 0$ terms on the left side and sets the right side to 0.

2.   Factor the equation. In order to factor, you generally need to think about two terms in the equation. Assuming that $a = 1$ (which is usually the case on GMAT quadratic equation problems), the two terms you should focus on are b and c. (If a is not equal to 1, simply divide the equation through by a.) The trick to factoring is to find two integers whose product equals c and whose sum equals b.

     In the equation $x^2 + 3x - 4 = 0$, we can see that $b = 3$ and $c = -4$. In order to factor this equation, we need to find two integers whose product is -4 and whose sum is 3. The only two integers that work are 4 and -1, since we can see that $4(-1) = -4$ and $4 + (-1) = 3$.

3.   Rewrite the equation in the form $(x + ?)(x + ?)$, where the question marks represent the two integers you solved for in the previous step.

     $x^2 + 3x - 4 = 0$
     $(x + 4)(x - 1) = 0$

Almost every quadratic equation on the GMAT can be factored. You will very rarely need to use the quadratic formula.

*Manhattan*GMAT*Prep

4.   The left side of the equation is now a product of two factors in parentheses: $(x + 4)$ and $(x − 1)$. **Since this product equals 0, one or both of the factors must be 0.** For instance, if we know that $M \times N = 0$, then we know that either $M = 0$ or $N = 0$ (or both M and N are zero).

In this problem, set each factor in parentheses independently to 0 and solve for x.

$x + 4 = 0$ OR $x − 1 = 0$ The two solutions for x have the
$x = −4$ $x = 1$ opposite signs of the integers we
                                                  found in step three.

Thus, the two solutions or roots of the quadratic equation $x^2 + 3x + 8 = 12$ are $−4$ and 1.

Beware of disguised
quadratics!

Disguised Quadratics

The GMAT will often attempt to disguise quadratic equations by putting them in forms that do not quite look like the traditional form of $ax^2 + bx + c = 0$.

Here is a very common "disguised" form for a quadratic: $3w^2 = 6w$

This is certainly a quadratic equation. However, it is very tempting to try to solve this equation without thinking of it as a quadratic. This classic mistake looks like this:

$3w^2 = 6w$ Dividing both sides by w and then dividing both sides by 3
$3w = 6$ yields the solution $w = 2$
$w = 2$

In solving this equation without factoring it like a quadratic, we have missed one of the solutions! Let us now solve it by factoring it as a quadratic equation:

$3w^2 = 6w$
$3w^2 − 6w = 0$
$w(3w − 6) = 0$

Setting both factors equal to 0 yields the following solutions:

$3w − 6 = 0$
$w = 0$ OR $3w = 6$
                              $w = 2$

In recognizing that $3w^2 = 6w$ is a disguised quadratic, we have found both solutions instead of accidentally missing one (in this case, the solution $w = 0$).

Here is another example of a disguised quadratic:

Solve for b, given that $\dfrac{36}{b} = b − 5$.

At first glance, this does not look like a quadratic equation, but once we begin solving the equation we should recognize that it is a quadratic.

$\dfrac{36}{b} = b - 5$ We start by multiplying both sides of the equation by b. After we do this, we should recognize the components of

$36 = b^2 - 5b$ a quadratic equation.

Now we should treat this as a quadratic equation and solve it by factoring:

$36 = b^2 - 5b$
$b^2 - 5b - 36 = 0$
$(b - 9)(b + 4) = 0$ Thus, $b = 9$ or $b = -4$.

Some quadratics are hidden within more difficult equations, such as higher order equations (in which a variable is raised to the power of 3 or more). On the GMAT, these equations can almost always be factored to find the hidden quadratic expression. For example:

Solve for x, given that $x^3 + 2x^2 - 3x = 0$.

$x^3 + 2x^2 - 3x = 0$ In factoring out an x from each term, we are left with the
$x(x^2 + 2x - 3) = 0$ product of x and the quadratic expression $x^2 + 2x - 3$.

Now we can factor the hidden quadratic:

$x(x^2 + 2x - 3) = 0$
$x(x + 3)(x - 1) = 0$ We have a product of three factors: x, $(x + 3)$, and $(x - 1)$. This product equals 0. Thus, one of the factors equals 0. That is, either $x = 0$ OR $x + 3 = 0$ OR $x - 1 = 0$. This equation has *three* solutions: 0, -3, and 1.

From this example, we can learn a general rule:

If you have a quadratic expression equal to 0, *and* you can factor an x out of the expression, then $x = 0$ is a solution of the equation.

Be careful not to just divide both sides by x. This division improperly eliminates the solution $x = 0$. You are only allowed to divide by a variable (or ANY expression) if you are absolutely sure that the variable or expression does not equal zero. (After all, you cannot divide by zero, even in theory.)

Manipulations can help you uncover disguised quadratics.

Going in Reverse: Use FOIL

Instead of starting with a quadratic equation and factoring it, you may need to start with factors and rewrite them as a quadratic equation. To do this, you need to use a multiplication process called FOIL: First, Outer, Inner, Last.

To change the expression $(x + 7)(x - 3)$ into a quadratic equation, use FOIL as follows:

First: Multiply the <u>first term</u> of each factor together: $x \cdot x = x^2$

Outer: Multiply the <u>outer terms</u> of the expression together: $x(-3) = -3x$

Inner: Multiply the <u>inner terms</u> of the expression together: $7(x) = 7x$

Last: Multiply the <u>last term</u> of each factor together: $7(-3) = -21$

Now, there are 4 terms: $x^2 - 3x + 7x - 21$. By combining the two middle terms, we have our quadratic expression: $x^2 + 4x - 21$.

Notice that FOIL is equivalent to distribution:
$$(x + 7)(x - 3) = x(x - 3) + 7(x - 3) = x^2 - 3x + 7x - 21.$$

If you encounter a quadratic equation, try factoring it. On the other hand, if you encounter the product of factors such as $(x + 7)(x - 3)$, you may need to use FOIL. Note: if the product of factors equals zero, then be ready to *interpret* the meaning. For instance, if you are given $(x + k)(x - m) = 0$, then you know that $x = -k$ or $x = m$.

Using FOIL with Square Roots

Some GMAT problems ask you to solve factored expressions that involve roots. For example, the GMAT might ask you to solve the following:

What is the value of $(\sqrt{8} - \sqrt{3})(\sqrt{8} + \sqrt{3})$?

Even though these problems do not involve any variables, you can solve them just like you would solve a pair of quadratic factors: use FOIL.

FIRST: $\sqrt{8} \cdot \sqrt{8} = 8$ OUTER: $\sqrt{8} \cdot \sqrt{3} = \sqrt{24}$

INNER: $\sqrt{8} \cdot \left(-\sqrt{3}\right) = -\sqrt{24}$ LAST: $\left(-\sqrt{3}\right)\left(\sqrt{3}\right) = -3$

The 4 terms are: $8 + \sqrt{24} - \sqrt{24} - 3$.

We can simplify this expression by removing the two middle terms (they cancel each other out) and subtracting: $8 + \sqrt{24} - \sqrt{24} - 3 = 8 - 3 = 5$. Although the problem looks complex, using FOIL reduces the entire expression to 5.

Reversing the process is generally an effective first step towards a solution. Factoring and distributing (using FOIL) are reverse processes.

ManhattanGMAT Prep

One-Solution Quadratics

Not all quadratic equations have two solutions. Some have only one solution. One-solution quadratics are also called **perfect square** quadratics, because both roots are the same. Consider the following examples:

$$x^2 + 8x + 16 = 0$$
$$(x + 4)(x + 4) = 0$$
$$(x + 4)^2 = 0 \qquad \text{Here, the only solution for } x \text{ is } -4.$$

$$x^2 - 6x + 9 = 0$$
$$(x - 3)(x - 3) = 0$$
$$(x - 3)^2 = 0 \qquad \text{Here, the only solution for } x \text{ is } 3.$$

Be careful not to assume that a quadratic equation always has two solutions. Always factor quadratic equations to determine their solutions. In doing so, you will see whether a quadratic equation has one or two solutions.

Zero In the Denominator: Undefined

Math convention does not allow division by 0. When 0 appears in the denominator of an expression, then that expression is undefined. How does this convention affect quadratic equations? Consider the following:

What are the solutions to the following equation?

$$\frac{x^2 + x - 12}{x - 2} = 0$$

We notice a quadratic equation in the numerator. Since it is a good idea to start solving quadratic equations by factoring, we will factor this numerator as follows:

$$\frac{x^2 + x - 12}{x - 2} = 0 \rightarrow \frac{(x - 3)(x + 4)}{x - 2} = 0$$

If either of the factors in the numerator is 0, then the entire expression becomes 0. Thus, the solutions to this equation are $x = 3$ or $x = -4$.

Note that making the denominator of the fraction equal to 0 would NOT make the entire expression equal to 0. Recall that if 0 appears in the denominator, the expression becomes undefined. Thus, $x = 2$ (which would make the denominator equal to 0) is NOT a solution to this equation. In fact, since setting x equal to 2 would make the denominator 0, the value 2 is illegal: x **cannot** equal 2.

A fraction can NEVER have a denominator of zero.

The Three Special Products

Three quadratic expressions called *special products* come up so frequently on the GMAT that it pays to memorize them. They are GMAT favorites! You should immediately recognize these 3 expressions and know how to factor (or distribute) each one automatically. This will usually put you on the path toward the solution to the problem.

Special Product #1: $x^2 - y^2 = (x + y)(x - y)$

Special Product #2: $x^2 + 2xy + y^2 = (x + y)(x + y) = (x + y)^2$

Special Product #3: $x^2 - 2xy + y^2 = (x - y)(x - y) = (x - y)^2$

> When you see one of these special products, factor (or distribute) it immediately.

You should be able to identify these products when they are presented in disguised form. For example, $a^2 - 1$ can be factored as $(a + 1)(a - 1)$. Similarly, $(a + b)^2$ can be distributed as $a^2 + 2ab + b^2$.

Within an equation, you may need to recognize these special products in pieces. For instance, if you see $a^2 + b^2 = 9 + 2ab$, move the $2ab$ term to the left, yielding $a^2 + b^2 - 2ab = 9$. This quadratic can then be factored to $(a - b)^2 = 9$, or $a - b = \pm 3$.

> Simplify: $\dfrac{x^2 + 4x + 4}{x^2 - 4}$, given that x does not equal 2 or −2.

Both the numerator and denominator of this fraction can be factored:

$$\frac{(x + 2)(x + 2)}{(x + 2)(x - 2)}$$ The numerator of the fraction is Special Product #2.
The denominator of the fraction is Special Product #1.

The expression $x + 2$ can be cancelled out from the numerator and denominator:

$$\frac{x^2 + 4x + 4}{x^2 - 4} = \frac{x + 2}{x - 2}$$

Notice that we could NOT simplify this expression if we were not told that $x \neq -2$. If $x = -2$, the expression on the left would be undefined (division by zero), whereas the expression on the right would equal 0. Thankfully, the GMAT often rules out illegal values (such as −2 in this example) that would cause division by zero.

Avoid the following common mistakes with special products:

Wrong: $(x + y)^2 = x^2 + y^2$?   Right: $(x + y)^2 = x^2 + 2xy + y^2$
                    $(x - y)^2 = x^2 - y^2$? $(x - y)^2 = x^2 - 2xy + y^2$

Problem Set

Solve the following problems. Distribute and factor when needed.

1. If -4 is a solution for x in the equation $x^2 + kx + 8 = 0$, what is k?

2. Given that $\dfrac{d}{4} + \dfrac{8}{d} + 3 = 0$, what is d?

3. If 8 and -4 are the solutions for x, which of the following could be the equation?
    (A) $x^2 - 4x - 32 = 0$ (B) $x^2 - 4x + 32 = 0$ (C) $x^2 + 4x - 12 = 0$
    (D) $x^2 + 4x + 32 = 0$ (E) $x^2 + 4x + 12 = 0$

4. Given that $\dfrac{x^2 + 6x + 9}{x + 3} = 7$, what is x?

5. Given that $16 - y^2 = 10(4 + y)$, what is y?

6. Given that $x^2 - 10 = -1$, what is x?

7. Given that $\dfrac{(x + y)(x - y) + y^2}{8} = 2$, what is x?

8. Given that $x^2 - 13x = 30$, what is x?

9. If $x^2 + k = G$ and x is an integer, which of the following could be the value of $G - k$?
    (A) 7   (B) 8   (C) 9   (D) 10   (E) 11

10. If the area of a certain square (expressed in square meters) is added to its perimeter (expressed in meters), the sum is 77. What is the length of a side of the square?

11. Hugo lies on top of a building, throwing pennies straight down to the street below. The formula for the height, H, that a penny falls is $H = Vt + 5t^2$, where V is the original velocity of the penny (how fast Hugo throws it when it leaves his hand) and t is equal to the time it takes to hit the ground. The building is 60 meters high, and Hugo throws the penny down at an initial speed of 20 meters per second. How long does it take for the penny to hit the ground?

12. $(3 - \sqrt{7})(3 + \sqrt{7}) =$

13. If $x^2 - 6x - 27 = 0$ and $y^2 - 6y - 40 = 0$, what is the maximum value of $x + y$?

14. Given that $x^2 - 10x + 25 = 16$, what is x?

15. Data Sufficiency: What is x?
    (1) $x = 4y - 4$ (2) $xy = 8$

1. $k = 6$: If -4 is a solution, then we know that $(x + 4)$ must be one of the factors of the quadratic equation. The other factor is $(x + ?)$. We know that the product of 4 and ? must be equal to 8; thus, the other factor is $(x + 2)$. We know that the sum of 4 and 2 must be equal to k. Therefore, $k = 6$.

2. $d = \{-8, -4\}$: Multiply the entire equation by $4d$ (to eliminate the denominators) and factor.

$$d^2 + 32 + 12d = 0$$
$$d^2 + 12d + 32 = 0$$
$$(d + 8)(d + 4) = 0$$

$$d + 8 = 0 \qquad \text{OR} \qquad d + 4 = 0$$
$$d = -8 \qquad\qquad\qquad d = -4$$

3. **(A)**: If the solutions to the equation are 8 and -4, the factored form of the equation is:
$$(x - 8)(x + 4)$$

Use FOIL to find the quadratic form: $x^2 - 4x - 32$. Therefore, the correct equation is (A).

4. $x = 4$: Cross-multiply, simplify, and factor to solve.
$$\frac{x^2 + 6x + 9}{x + 3} = 7$$

$$x^2 + 6x + 9 = 7x + 21$$
$$x^2 - x - 12 = 0$$
$$(x + 3)(x - 4) = 0$$

$$x + 3 = 0 \qquad \text{OR} \qquad x - 4 = 0$$
$$x = -3 \qquad\qquad\qquad x = 4$$

Discard -3 as a value for x, since this value would make the denominator zero; thus, the fraction would be undefined.

5. $y = \{-4, -6\}$: Simplify and factor to solve.
$$16 - y^2 = 10(4 + y)$$
$$16 - y^2 = 40 + 10y$$
$$y^2 + 10y + 24 = 0$$
$$(y + 4)(y + 6) = 0$$

$$y + 4 = 0 \qquad \text{OR} \qquad y + 6 = 0$$
$$y = -4 \qquad\qquad\qquad y = -6$$

Notice that it is possible to factor the left-hand side of the equation first: $16 - y^2 = (4 + y)(4 - y)$.

However, doing so is potentially dangerous: you may decide to then divide both sides of the equation by $(4 + y)$. You cannot do this, because it is possible that $(4 + y)$ equals zero!

*Manhattan*GMAT®Prep
the new standard

6. $x = \{-3, 3\}$:
$$x^2 - 10 = -1$$
$$x^2 = 9$$
$$x = \{-3, 3\}$$

7. $x = \{-4, 4\}$:
$$\frac{(x + y)(x - y) + y^2}{8} = 2$$
$$(x + y)(x - y) + y^2 = 16$$
$$x^2 - y^2 + y^2 = 16$$
$$x^2 = 16$$
$$x = \{-4, 4\}$$

8. $x = \{15, -2\}$:
$$x^2 - 13x = 30$$
$$x^2 - 13x - 30 = 0$$
$$(x + 2)(x - 15) = 0$$

$x + 2 = 0$ OR $x - 15 = 0$
       $x = -2$ OR $x = 15$

9. **(C)**: $x^2 + k = G$
               $x^2 = G - k$

In order for x to be an integer, $G - k$ must be a perfect square. The only perfect square among the answer choices is (C) 9.

10. $s = 7$: The area of the square $= s^2$. The perimeter of the square $= 4s$.
$$s^2 + 4s = 77$$
$$s^2 + 4s - 77 = 0$$
$$(s + 11)(s - 7) = 0$$

$s + 11 = 0$ OR $s - 7 = 0$ Since the edge of a square must be positive,
       $s = -11$ $s = 7$ discard the negative value for s.

11. $t = 2$:
$$H = Vt + 5t^2$$
$$60 = 20t + 5t^2$$
$$5t^2 + 20t - 60 = 0$$
$$5(t^2 + 4t - 12) = 0$$
$$5(t + 6)(t - 2) = 0$$

$t + 6 = 0$ OR $t - 2 = 0$ Since a time must be positive, discard the
       $t = -6$ $t = 2$ negative value for t.

12. **2:** Use FOIL to simplify this product:

F: $3 \times 3 = 9$
O: $3 \times \sqrt{7} = 3\sqrt{7}$
I: $-\sqrt{7} \times 3 = -3\sqrt{7}$
L: $-\sqrt{7} \times \sqrt{7} = -7$
$9 + 3\sqrt{7} - 3\sqrt{7} - 7 = 2$

Alternatively, recognize that the original expression is in the form $(x - y)(x + y)$, which is one of the three special products and which equals $x^2 - y^2$ (the difference of two squares). Thus, the expression simplifies to $3^2 - (\sqrt{7})^2 = 9 - 7 = 2$.

13. **19:** Factor both quadratic equations. Then, use the largest possible values of x and y to find the maximum value of the sum $x + y$.

$$x^2 - 6x - 27 = 0 \qquad\qquad y^2 - 6y - 40 = 0$$
$$(x + 3)(x - 9) = 0 \qquad\qquad (y + 4)(y - 10) = 0$$

$x + 3 = 0$ OR $x - 9 = 0$ $y + 4 = 0$ OR $y - 10 = 0$
    $x = -3$ $x = 9$ $y = -4$ $y = 10$

The maximum possible value of $x + y = 9 + 10 = 19$.

14. **$x = \{1, 9\}$:**

$$x^2 - 10x + 25 = 16$$
$$x^2 - 10x + 9 = 0$$
$$(x - 9)(x - 1) = 0$$

$x - 9 = 0$ OR $x - 1 = 0$
    $x = 9$ $x = 1$

15. **(E) Statements 1 and 2 TOGETHER are NOT SUFFICIENT:** Each statement alone is not enough information to solve for x. Using statements 1 and 2 combined, if we substitute the expression for x in the first equation, into the second, we get two different answers:

$x = 4y - 4$ $(y + 1)(y - 2) = 0$

$xy = (4y - 4)y = 8$ $y = \{-1, 2\}$

$4y^2 - 4y = 8$ $\boldsymbol{x = \{-8, 4\}}$

$y^2 - y - 2 = 0$

Chapter 4
of

EQUATIONS, INEQUALITIES, & VICs

FORMULAS

In This Chapter . . .

FORMULAS

Formulas are another means by which the GMAT tests your ability to work with unknowns. Formulas are specific equations that can involve multiple variables. There are 4 major types of Formula problems which the GMAT tests:

(1) Plug-in Formulas
(2) Strange Symbol Formulas
(3) Formulas with Unspecified Amounts
(4) Sequence Formulas

The GMAT uses formulas both in abstract problems and in real-life word problems. Becoming adept at working with formulas of all kinds is critical to your GMAT success.

Plug-In Formulas

The most basic GMAT formula problems provide you with a formula and ask you to solve for one of the variables in the formula by plugging in given values for the other variables. For example:

> The formula for determining an individual's comedic aptitude, C, on a given day is defined as $\dfrac{QL}{J}$, where J represents the number of jokes told, Q represents the overall joke quality on a scale of 1 to 10, and L represents the number of individual laughs generated. If Nicole told 12 jokes, generated 18 laughs, and earned a comedic aptitude of 10.5, what was the overall quality of her jokes?

Solving this problem simply involves plugging the given values into the formula in order to solve for the unknown variable Q:

$$C = \frac{QL}{J} \;\rightarrow\; 10.5 = \frac{18Q}{12} \;\rightarrow\; 10.5(12) = 18Q \;\rightarrow\; Q = \frac{10.5(12)}{18} \;\rightarrow\; Q = 7$$

The quality of Nicole's jokes was rated a 7.

Notice that you will typically have to do some rearrangement after plugging in the numbers, in order to isolate the desired unknown. The actual computations are not complex. What makes Formula problems tricky is the unfamiliarity of the given formula, which may seem to come from "out of the blue." Do not be intimidated. Simply write the equation down, plug in the numbers carefully, and solve for the required unknown.

Be sure to write the formula as a part of an equation. For instance, do not just write "$\dfrac{QL}{J}$" on your paper. Rather, write "$C = \dfrac{QL}{J}$." Look for language such as "is defined as" to identify what equals what.

Manhattan **GMAT** *Prep*
the new standard

Strange Symbol Formulas

Another type of GMAT formula problem involves the use of strange symbols. In these problems, the GMAT introduces an arbitrary symbol, which defines a certain procedure. These problems may look confusing because of the unfamiliar symbols. However, the symbol is IRRELEVANT. All that is important is that you carefully follow each step in the procedure that the symbol indicates.

A technique that can be helpful is to break the operations down one by one and say them aloud (or in your head)—to "hear" them explicitly. Here are some examples:

FORMULA DEFINITION	STEP-BY-STEP BREAKDOWN
$x \heartsuit y = x^2 + y^2 - xy$	"The first number squared, plus the second number squared, minus the product of the two..."
$s \bigcirc t = (s - 2)(t + 2)$	"Two less than the first number times two more than the second number..."
$\boxed{x}$ is defined as the product of all integers smaller than x but greater than 0...	"...x minus 1, times x minus 2, times x minus 3... Aha! So this is $(x - 1)$ factorial!"

Notice that it can be helpful to refer to the variables as "the first number," "the second number," and so on. In this way, you use the physical position of the numbers to keep them straight in relation to the strange symbol.

Now that you have interpreted the formula step-by-step and can understand what it means, you can calculate a solution for the formula with actual numbers. Consider the following example:

$$W \Psi F = \left(\sqrt{W}\right)^F \text{ for all integers } W \text{ and } F. \text{ What is } 4 \Psi 9 ?$$

The symbol Ψ between two numbers signals the following procedure: take the square root of the first number and then raise that value to the power of the second number.

$$4 \Psi 9 = \left(\sqrt{4}\right)^9 = 2^9 = 512.$$

Watch out for symbols that INVERT the order of an operation. It is easy to automatically translate the function in a "left to right" manner even when that is NOT what the function specifies.

$$W \Phi F = \left(\sqrt{F}\right)^W \text{ for all integers } W \text{ and } F. \text{ What is } 4 \Phi 9?$$

It would be easy in this example to mistakenly calculate the formula in the same way as the first example. However notice that the order of the operation is REVERSED—we need to take the square root of the SECOND number, raised to the power of the FIRST number:

$$4 \Phi 9 = \left(\sqrt{9}\right)^4 = 3^4 = 81.$$

More challenging strange-symbol problems require you to use the given procedure more than once. For example:

$$W \Phi F = \left(\sqrt{F} \right)^{W}$$ for all integers W and F. What is $4 \Phi (3 \Phi 16)$?

Always perform the procedure inside the parentheses FIRST:

$$3 \Phi 16 = \left(\sqrt{16} \right)^{3} = 4^{3} = 64.$$

Now we can rewrite the original formula as follows: $4 \Phi (3 \Phi 16) = 4 \Phi 64$.

Performing the procedure a second time yields the answer:

$$4 \Phi 64 = \left(\sqrt{64} \right)^{4} = 8^{4} = 4,096.$$

Formulas with Unspecified Amounts

Some of the most challenging formula problems on the GMAT are those that involve unspecified amounts. Typically, these questions focus on the increase or decrease in the value of a certain formula, given a change in the value of the variables. Just as with other GMAT problems with unspecified amounts, solve these problems by PICKING NUMBERS!

> If the length of the side of a cube decreases by two-thirds, by what percentage will the volume of the cube decrease?

First, consider the formula involved here. The volume of a cube is defined by the formula $V = s^3$, where s represents the length of a side. Then, pick a number for the length of the side of the cube.

Let us say the cube has a side of 3 units. Note that this is a "smart" number to pick because it is divisible by 3 (the denominator of two-thirds).

Then, its volume $= s^3 = 3 \times 3 \times 3 = 27$.

If the cube's side decreases by two-thirds, its new length is $3 - \frac{2}{3}(3) = 1$ unit.

Its new volume $= s^3 = 1 \times 1 \times 1 = 1$.

We determine percentage decrease as follows:

$$\frac{\text{change}}{\text{original}} = \frac{27 - 1}{27} = \frac{26}{27} \approx 0.963 = 96.3\% \text{ decrease.}$$

Formula problems that involve unspecified amounts should be solved by picking smart numbers for the unspecified variables.

Sequence Formulas

The final type of GMAT formula problem involves sequences. A sequence is a collection of numbers in a set order. The order is determined by a RULE. Here are examples of sequence rules:

$A_n = 9n + 3$
(for $n \geq 1$)

The nth term of sequence A is defined by the rule $9n + 3$, for all integers $n \geq 1$. For example, the fourth term in this sequence, A_4, is $9n + 3 = 9(4) + 3 = 39$. The first five terms of the sequence are as follows, as you should verify for yourself:

12	21	30	39	48	...
A_1	A_2	A_3	A_4	A_5	...

By the way, when you see A_1, say "A-1" or "A sub 1," not "A to the 1." These subscripts are not exponents! They are just labels indicating which number in the sequence you are talking about.

$Q_n = n^2 + 4$
(for $n \geq 1$)

The nth term of sequence Q is defined by the rule $n^2 + 4$, for all integers $n \geq 1$. For example, the first term in this sequence, Q_1, is $1^2 + 4 = 5$. Verify the first five terms of the sequence:

5	8	13	20	29	...
Q_1	Q_2	Q_3	Q_4	Q_5	...

In the cases above, each item of the sequence is defined as a function of n, the place in which the term occurs in the sequence. For example, if you want to know the value of A_{100}, all you have to do is plug $n = 100$ into the **direct** definition of the sequence ($A_n = 9n + 3$).

> Sequences are defined by function rules: each term is a function of its place in the sequence.

Defining Rules for Sequences

An important thing to remember about sequence problems is that you MUST be given the rule in order to find a particular number in a sequence. It is tempting (but incorrect!) to try to solve sequence problems without the rule. For example:

If $S_7 = 5$ and $S_8 = 6$, what is S_9?

It seems as if this sequence counts upward by 1's, so it is tempting to say that $S_9 = 7$. However, this deduction is NOT valid, because we were not given the rule. The sequence might be 5, 6, 7, ... OR 5, 6, 28, ... Without the rule, there is no way to be sure.

A common sequence definition is a **linear** (or arithmetic) sequence. In these sequences, the difference between successive terms is always the same. The direct definition of a linear sequence is $S_n = kn + x$, where k is the constant difference between successive terms and x is some other constant.

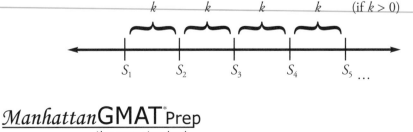

The first four terms of a sequence are 16, 20, 24, and 28, in that order. If the difference between each successive term is constant, what is the rule for this sequence?

Because we know that the difference between successive terms is the same, we know the sequence is linear. The difference between each term is 4, so this sequence must be in the form $4n + x$. We can find the value of x by using any of the terms in the sequence. In this example, the first term in the sequence ($n = 1$) has a value of 16, so $4(1) + x = 16$. Therefore, $x = 12$.

We can confirm that $x = 12$ by using another term in the sequence. For example, the second term in the sequence ($n = 2$) has a value of 20. This verifies that $x = 12$, since $4(2) + 12 = 20$. Therefore, $4n + 12$ is the rule for the sequence. We can use this formula to find any term in the sequence. $S_5 = 4 \cdot 5 + 12 = 32$; $S_6 = 4 \cdot 6 + 12 = 36$; etc.

Another common sequence definition is an **exponential** (or geometric) sequence. These sequences are of the form $S_n = x(k^n)$, where x and k are real numbers. Each term is equal to the previous term *times* a constant k. (In contrast, in a linear sequence, each term is equal to the previous term *plus* a constant k, as we saw earlier.)

The first four terms of a sequence are 20, 200, 2,000, and 20,000, in that order. If each term is equal to the previous term times a constant number, what is the rule for this sequence?

Because we know that each term is equal to the previous term times a constant number, we know the sequence is exponential. Each term is 10 times the previous term, so this sequence must be in the form $x(10^n)$. We can find the value of x by using any of the terms in the sequence. In this example, the first term in the sequence ($n = 1$) has a value of 20, so $x(10^1) = 20$. Therefore, $x = 2$. $S_1 = 2 \cdot 10^1 = 20$; $S_2 = 2 \cdot 10^2 = 200$; etc.

Sequence Problems: Alternate Method

For simple linear sequences, in which the same number is added to any term to yield the next term, you can use the following alternative method:

If each number in a sequence is three more than the previous number, and the sixth number is 32, what is the 100th number?

Instead of finding the rule for this sequence, consider the following reasoning:
From the sixth to the one hundredth term, there are 94 "jumps" of 3. Since $94 \times 3 = 282$, there is an increase of 282 from the sixth term to the one hundredth term:

$32 + 282 = 314$.

Linear sequences are of the form $kn + x$, where k equals the difference between successive terms.

Sequences and Patterns

Some sequences are easier to look at in terms of patterns, rather than rules. For example, consider the following:

If $S_n = 3^n$, what is the units digit of S_{65}?

Clearly, you cannot be expected to multiply out 3^{65} on the GMAT. Therefore, you must assume that there is a pattern in the powers of three.

$3^1 = \mathbf{3}$

$3^2 = \mathbf{9}$

$3^3 = 27$

$3^4 = 81$

$3^5 = 243$

$3^6 = 729$

$3^7 = 2,187$

$3^8 = 6,561$

Note the pattern of the units digits in the powers of 3: 3, 9, 7, 1, [repeating]... Also note that the units digit of S_n, when n is a multiple of 4, is always equal to 1. You can use the multiples of 4 as "anchor points" in the pattern. Since 65 is 1 more than 64 (the closest multiple of 4), the units digit of S_{65} will be 3, which always follows 1 in the pattern.

As a side note, most sequences on the GMAT are defined for integer $n \geq 1$. That is, the sequence S_n almost always starts at S_1. Occasionally, a sequence might start at S_0, but in that case, you are told that $n \geq 0$. Notice that the *first* term in the sequence would then be S_0, the *second* term would be S_1, the *third* term would be S_2, and so on.

Problem Set

1. Given that $A \lozenge B = 4A - B$, what is the value of $(3 \lozenge 2) \lozenge 3$?

2. Given that 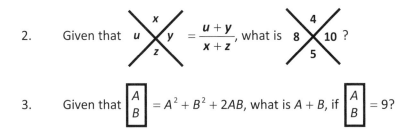 $= \dfrac{u + y}{x + z}$, what is $\;$?

3. Given that $\begin{array}{|c|} \hline A \\ \hline B \\ \hline \end{array} = A^2 + B^2 + 2AB$, what is $A + B$, if $\begin{array}{|c|} \hline A \\ \hline B \\ \hline \end{array} = 9$?

For problem #4, use the following information: $x \Longrightarrow y = x + (x + 1) + (x + 2) \ldots + y$.
For example, $3 \Longrightarrow 7 = 3 + 4 + 5 + 6 + 7$.

4. What is the value of $(100 \Longrightarrow 150) - (125 \Longrightarrow 150)$?

5. Life expectancy is defined by the formula $\dfrac{2SB}{G}$, where S = shoe size, B = average monthly electric bill in dollars, and G = GMAT score. If Melvin's GMAT score is twice his monthly electric bill, and his life expectancy is 50, what is his shoe size?

6. The formula for spring factor in a shoe insole is $\dfrac{w^2 + x}{3}$, where w is the width of the insole in centimeters and x is the grade of rubber on a scale of 1 to 9. What is the maximum spring factor for an insole that is 3 centimeters wide?

7. Cost is expressed by the formula tb^4. If b is doubled, by what factor has the cost increased?
   (A) 2   (B) 6   (C) 8   (D) 16   (E) ½

8. If the scale model of a cube sculpture is 0.5 cm per every 1 m of the real sculpture, what is the volume of the model, if the volume of the real sculpture is 64 m³?

9. The "competitive edge" of a baseball team is defined by the formula $\sqrt{\dfrac{W}{L}}$, where W represents the number of team's wins, and L represents the number of team's losses. This year, the GMAT All-Stars had 3 times as many wins and one-half as many losses as they had last year. By what factor did their "competitive edge" increase?

10. If the radius of a circle is tripled, what is the ratio of the area of half the original circle to the area of the whole new circle? (Area of a circle = πr^2, where r = radius)

11. If each number in a sequence is three more than the previous number, and the eighth number is 46, what is the rule for this sequence?

12.   If $S_n = 4^n + 5^{n+1} + 3$, what is the units digit of S_{100}?

13.   The first term in an arithmetic sequence is −5 and the second term is −3. What is the 50th term? (Recall that in an arithmetic sequence, the difference between successive terms is constant.)

For problems #14–15, use the following sequence: $A_n = 3 - 8n$.

14.   What is A_1?

15.   What is $A_{11} - A_9$?

1. **37:** First, simplify 3 ◊ 2: 4(3) − 2 = 12 − 2 = 10. Then, solve 10 ◊ 3: 4(10) − 3 = 40 − 3 = 37.

2. **2:** Plug the numbers in the grid into the formula, matching up the number in each section with the corresponding variable in the formula $\dfrac{u+y}{x+z} = \dfrac{8+10}{4+5} = \dfrac{18}{9} = 2$.

3. **A + B = {3, −3}:**

$$A^2 + B^2 + 2AB = 9$$
$$(A + B)^2 = 9$$
$$A + B = 3 \quad \text{OR} \quad A + B = -3$$

First, set the formula equal to 9. Then, factor the expression $A^2 + B^2 + 2AB$. Unsquare both sides, taking both the positive and negative roots into account.

4. **2,800:** This problem contains two components: the sum of all the numbers from 100 to 150, and the sum of all the numbers from 125 to 150. Since we are finding the difference between these two components, we are essentially finding just the sum of all the numbers from 100 to 124. You can think of this logically by solving a simpler problem: find the difference between (1 ==> 5) − (3 ==> 5).

$$
\begin{array}{r}
1 + 2 + 3 + 4 + 5 \\
-\qquad\quad 3 + 4 + 5 \\
\hline
1 + 2 \qquad\qquad\quad
\end{array}
$$

There are 25 numbers from 100 to 124 (124 − 100 + 1). Remember to add one before you are done! To find the sum of these numbers, multiply by the average term: (100 + 124) ÷ 2 = 112. 25 × 112 = 2,800.

5. **Size 50:**

$$\frac{2SB}{2B} = 50$$
$$S = 50$$

Substitute 2B for G in the formula. Note that the term 2B appears in both the numerator and denominator, so they cancel out.

6. **6:** Determine the maximum spring factor by setting $x = 9$.

Let s = spring factor

$$s = \frac{w^2 + x}{3} \qquad\qquad s = \frac{(3)^2 + 9}{3} = \frac{18}{3} = 6$$

7. **(D):** Pick numbers to see what happens to the cost when b is doubled. If the original value of b is 2, the cost is $16t$. When b is doubled to 4, the new cost value is $256t$. The cost has increased by a factor of $\dfrac{256}{16}$, or 16.

8. **8 cm³:**

$$V = s^3 \;\rightarrow\; 64 = s^3 \;\rightarrow\; s = 4$$

The length of a side on the real sculpture is 4 m.

$$\frac{0.5 \text{ cm}}{1 \text{ m}} = \frac{x \text{ cm}}{4 \text{ m}} \;\rightarrow\; x = 2$$

The length of a side on the model is 2 cm.

$$V = s^3 = (2)^3 = 8$$

The volume of the model is 8 cm³.

9. $\sqrt{6}$:

Let c = competitive edge

$$c = \sqrt{\frac{W}{L}}$$

Pick numbers to see what happens to the competitive edge when W is tripled and L is halved. If the original value of W is 2 and the original value of L is 4, the original value of c is

$\sqrt{\frac{2}{4}} = \sqrt{\frac{1}{2}} = \frac{1}{\sqrt{2}} = \frac{\sqrt{2}}{2}$. If W triples to 6 and L is halved to 2, the new value of c is $\sqrt{\frac{6}{2}} = \sqrt{3}$.

The competitive edge has increased from $\frac{\sqrt{2}}{2}$ to $\sqrt{3}$.

$$\frac{\sqrt{2}}{2}x = \sqrt{3} \qquad\qquad \frac{\sqrt{2}}{2}x = \sqrt{3}\left(\frac{2}{\sqrt{2}}\right) = \frac{2\sqrt{3}}{\sqrt{2}} = \frac{2\sqrt{3}\left(\sqrt{2}\right)}{2} = \sqrt{6}$$

The competitive edge has increased by a factor of $\sqrt{6}$.

10. $\frac{1}{18}$:

Pick real numbers to solve this problem. Set the radius of the original circle equal to 2. Therefore, the radius of the new circle is equal to 6. Once you compute the areas of both circles, you can find the ratio:

Original Circle	New Circle
$r = 2$	$r = 6$
$A = \pi r^2$	$A = \pi r^2$
$= 4\pi$	$= 36\pi$

$$\frac{\text{Area of half the original circle}}{\text{Area of the new circle}} = \frac{2\pi}{36\pi} = \frac{1}{18}$$

11. **$3n + 22$:** Set up a partial sequence table in order to derive the rule for this sequence. Because the difference between successive terms in the sequence is always 3, you know that the rule will be of the form $3n + x$. You can then solve for x using any term in the sequence. Using the fact that the 8th term has a value of 46, we know that $3(8) + x = 46$. Thus, $x = 22$ and the rule for this sequence is $3n + 22$.

n	value
6	40
7	43
8	46
9	49

12. **4:** Begin by listing the first few terms in the sequence, so that you can find a pattern:

$S_1 = 4^1 + 5^{1+1} + 3 = 4 + 25 + 3 = \mathbf{32}$
$S_2 = 4^2 + 5^{2+1} + 3 = 16 + 125 + 3 = \mathbf{144}$
$S_3 = 4^3 + 5^{3+1} + 3 = 64 + 625 + 3 = \mathbf{692}$
$S_4 = 4^4 + 5^{4+1} + 3 = 256 + 3{,}125 + 3 = \mathbf{3{,}384}$

The units digit of all odd-numbered terms is 2. The units digit of all even-numbered terms is 4. Since S_{100} is an even-numbered term, its units digit will be 4.

*Manhattan*GMAT·Prep
the new standard

An alternative solution method is to find the units digit of each term by using the respective patterns for that term, and then add them together (paying attention only to the units digit as you add). The 4^n pattern repeats every two terms: $4^1 = $ **4**, $4^2 = $ **16**, $4^3 = $ **64**, $4^4 = $ **256**, etc. The 5^n pattern is very easy: every power of 5 ends in **5**. Additionally, **3** will always be the same regardless of n. Therefore the pattern is that when n is odd, the units digit of S_n will be $4 + 5 + 3 = $ **12**, or 2. When n is even, the units digit of S_n will be $6 + 5 + 3 = $ **14**, or 4.

13. **93:** We know that the first term is -5, and there are $50 - 1 = 49$ "jumps" to get to the 50th term. Each "jump" is 2 units (which is the difference between the first and second terms), so $-5 + (2)(50 - 1) = 93$.

14. **−5:** $A_n = 3 - 8n$
$A_1 = 3 - 8(1) = 3 - 8 = -5$

15. **−16:** $A_n = 3 - 8n$
$A_{11} = 3 - 8(11) = 3 - 88 = -85$
$A_9 = 3 - 8(9) = 3 - 72 = -69$
$A_{11} - A_9 = -85 - (-69) = -16$

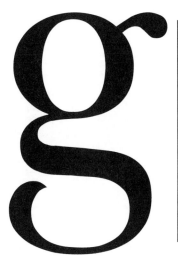

Chapter 5

of

EQUATIONS, INEQUALITIES, & VICs

FUNCTIONS

In This Chapter . . .

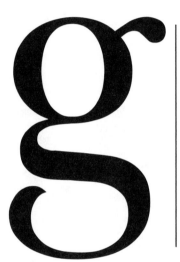

- Numerical Substitution
- Variable Substitution
- Compound Functions
- Functions with Unknown Constants
- Function Graphs
- Common Function Types

FUNCTIONS

Functions are very much like the "magic boxes" you may have learned about in elementary school.

> You put a 2 into the magic box, and a 7 comes out. You put a 3 into the magic box, and a 9 comes out. You put a 4 into the magic box, and an 11 comes out. What is the magic box doing to your number?

There are many possible ways to describe what the magic box is doing to your number. One possibility is as follows: The magic box is doubling your number and adding 3.

$$2(2) + 3 = 7 \qquad\qquad 2(3) + 3 = 9 \qquad\qquad 2(4) + 3 = 11$$

Assuming that this is the case (it is possible that the magic box is actually doing something different to your number), this description would yield the following "rule" for this magic box: $2x + 3$. This rule can be written in function form as:

$$f(x) = 2x + 3.$$

The function f represents the "rule" that the magic box is using to transform your number. Again, this rule may or may not be the "true" rule for the magic box. That is, if we put more numbers into the box and watch what numbers emerge, this rule may or may not hold. It is never possible to generalize a rule only by using specific cases.

Nevertheless, the magic box analogy is a helpful way to conceptualize a function as a RULE built on an independent variable. The value of a function changes as the value of the independent variable changes. In other words, the value of a function is dependent on the value of the independent variable. Examples of functions include:

$f(x) = 4x^2 - 11$ — The value of the function, f, is dependent on the independent variable, x.

$g(t) = t^3 + \sqrt{t} - \dfrac{2t}{5}$ — The value of the function, g, is dependent on the independent variable, t.

We can think of functions as consisting of an "input" variable (the number you put into the magic box), and a corresponding "output" value (the number that comes out of the box). The function is simply the rule that turns the "input" variable into the "output" variable.

By the way, the expression $f(x)$ is pronounced "f of x", not "fx." It does NOT mean "f TIMES x"! The letter f does NOT stand for a variable; rather, it stands for the rule that dictates how the input x changes into the output $f(x)$.

The "domain" of a function indicates the possible inputs. The "range" of a function indicates the possible outputs. For instance, the function $f(x) = x^2$ can take any input but never produces a negative number. So the domain is all numbers, but the range is $f(x) \geq 0$.

> A function rule describes a series of operations to perform on a variable.

Numerical Substitution

This is the most basic type of function problem. Input the numerical value (say, 5) in place of the independent variable (x) to determine the value of the function.

> If $f(x) = x^2 - 2$, what is the value of $f(5)$?

In this problem, you are given a rule for $f(x)$: square x and subtract 2. Then, you are asked to apply this rule to the number 5. Square 5 and subtract 2 from the result:

$$f(5) = (5)^2 - 2 = 25 - 2 = 23$$

Variable Substitution

This type of problem is slightly more complicated. Instead of finding the output value for a numerical input, you must find the output when the input is an algebraic expression.

> If $f(z) = z^2 - \dfrac{z}{3}$, what is the value of $f(w + 6)$?

Input the variable expression ($w + 6$) in place of the independent variable (z) to determine the value of the function:

$$f(w + 6) = (w + 6)^2 - \frac{w + 6}{3}$$

Compare this equation to the equation for $f(z)$. The expression ($w + 6$) has taken the place of every z in the original equation. In a sense, you are treating the expression ($w + 6$) as one thing, as if it were a single letter or variable.

The rest is algebraic simplification:

$$f(w + 6) = (w + 6)(w + 6) - \left(\frac{w}{3} + \frac{6}{3} \right)$$
$$= w^2 + 12w + 36 - \frac{w}{3} - 2$$
$$= w^2 + 11\frac{2}{3}w + 34$$

When substituting a variable expression into a function, keep the expression inside parentheses.

Compound Functions

Imagine putting a number into one magic box, and then putting the output directly into another magic box. This is the situation you have with compound functions.

If $f(x) = x^3 + \sqrt{x}$ and $g(x) = 4x - 3$, what is $f(g(3))$?

The expression $f(g(3))$, pronounced "f of g of 3", looks ugly, but the key to solving compound function problems is to work from the INSIDE OUT. In this case, start with $g(3)$. Notice that we put the number into g, not into f, which may seem backward at first.

$$g(3) = 4(3) - 3 = 12 - 3 = 9$$

Use the result from the <u>inner</u> function g as the new input variable for the <u>outer</u> function f:

$$f(g(3)) = f(9) = (9)^3 + \sqrt{9} = 729 + 3 = 732 \qquad \text{The final result is 732.}$$

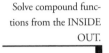

Solve compound functions from the INSIDE OUT.

Note that changing the order of the compound functions changes the answer:

If $f(x) = x^3 + \sqrt{x}$ and $g(x) = 4x - 3$, what is $g(f(3))$?

Again, work from the inside out. This time, start with $f(3)$ [which is now the inner function]:

$$f(3) = (3)^3 + \sqrt{3} = 27 + \sqrt{3}$$

Use the result from the <u>inner</u> function f as the new input variable for the <u>outer</u> function g:

$$g(f(3)) = g(27 + \sqrt{3}) = 4(27 + \sqrt{3}) - 3 = 108 + 4\sqrt{3} - 3 = 105 + 4\sqrt{3}$$

Thus, $g(f(3)) = 105 + 4\sqrt{3}$.

In general, $f(g(x))$ and $g(f(x))$ are **not the same rule overall** and will often lead to different outcomes. As an analogy, think of "putting on socks" and "putting on shoes" as two functions: the order in which you perform these steps obviously matters!

You may be asked to <u>find</u> a value of x for which $f(g(x)) = g(f(x))$. In that case, use <u>variable substitution</u>, working as always from the inside out:

If $f(x) = x^3 + 1$, and $g(x) = 2x$, for what value of x does $f(g(x)) = g(f(x))$?

Simply evaluate as we did in the problems above, using x instead of an input value:

$$f(g(x)) = g(f(x))$$
$$f(2x) = g(x^3 + 1)$$
$$(2x)^3 + 1 = 2(x^3 + 1)$$

$$8x^3 + 1 = 2x^3 + 2$$
$$6x^3 = 1$$
$$x = \sqrt[3]{\frac{1}{6}}$$

FUNCTIONS STRATEGY

Functions with Unknown Constants

On the GMAT, you may be given a function with an unknown constant. You will also be given the value of the function for a specific number. You can combine these pieces of information to find the complete function rule.

> If $f(x) = ax^2 - x$, and $f(4) = 28$, what is $f(-2)$?

Solve these problems in three steps. FIRST, use the value of the input variable and the corresponding output value of the function to solve for the unknown constant:

$$f(4) = a(4)^2 - 4 = 28$$
$$16a - 4 = 28$$
$$16a = 32$$
$$a = 2$$

THEN, rewrite the function, replacing the constant with its numerical value:

$$f(x) = ax^2 - x = 2x^2 - x$$

FINALLY, solve the function for the new input variable:

$$f(-2) = 2(-2)^2 - (-2) = 8 + 2 = 10$$

Function Graphs

A function can be visualized by graphing it in the coordinate plane. The input variable is considered the domain of the function, or the x-coordinate. The corresponding output is considered the range of the function, or the y-coordinate.

> What is the graph of the function $f(x) = -2x^2 + 1$?

Create an INPUT-OUTPUT table by evaluating the function for several input values:

INPUT	OUTPUT	(x, y)
−3	$-2(-3)^2 + 1 = -17$	$(-3, -17)$
−2	$-2(-2)^2 + 1 = -7$	$(-2, -7)$
−1	$-2(-1)^2 + 1 = -1$	$(-1, -1)$
0	$-2(0)^2 + 1 = 1$	$(0, 1)$
1	$-2(1)^2 + 1 = -1$	$(1, -1)$
2	$-2(2)^2 + 1 = -7$	$(2, -7)$
3	$-2(3)^2 + 1 = -17$	$(3, -17)$

Then, plot points to see the shape of the graph:

For more on graphing functions, see the "Coordinate Plane" chapter of the Manhattan GMAT *Geometry* Strategy Guide.

> The key to identifying function graphs is plotting points.

*Manhattan*GMAT*Prep
the new standard

Common Function Types

Though the GMAT could pose function questions in many different forms, several different themes occur through many of them. This section explores some of these common types of functions.

PROPORTIONALITY

Many GMAT problems, especially those concerned with real-life situations, will use direct or inverse proportionality between the input and the output values. These special functions are defined as follows.

Direct proportionality means that the two quantities always change by the same factor and in the same direction. For instance, tripling the input will cause the output to triple as well. Cutting the input in half will also cut the output in half. Direct proportionality relationships are of the form $y = kx$, where x is the input value and y is the output value. k is called

the **proportionality constant**. This equation can also be written as $\frac{y}{x} = k$, which means

that the ratio of the output and input values is always constant.

> The maximum height reached by an object thrown directly upward is directly proportional to the square of the velocity with which the object is thrown. If an object thrown upward at 16 feet per second reaches a maximum height of 4 feet, with what speed must the object be thrown upward to reach a maximum height of 9 feet?

Typically with direct proportion problems, you will be given "before" and "after" values.

Simply set up ratios to solve the problem—for example, $\frac{y_1}{x_1}$ can be used for the "before"

values and $\frac{y_2}{x_2}$ can be used for the "after" values. We then write $\frac{y_1}{x_1} = \frac{y_2}{x_2}$, since both ratios

are equal to the same constant k. Finally, we solve for the unknowns.

In the problem given above, be sure to note that the direct proportion is between the height and the *square* of the velocity, not the velocity itself. Therefore, write the proportion as

$\frac{h_1}{v_1^2} = \frac{h_2}{v_2^2}$. Substitute the known values $h_1 = 4$, $v_1 = 16$, and $h_2 = 9$:

$$\frac{4}{16^2} = \frac{9}{v_2^2} \qquad v_2^2 = 9\left(\frac{16^2}{4}\right) \qquad v_2^2 = 9(64) = 576 \qquad v_2 = 24$$

The object must be thrown upward at 24 feet per second.

Inverse proportionality means that the two quantities change by RECIPROCAL factors. Cutting the input in half will actually double the output. Tripling the input will cut the output to one-third of its original value.

Inverse proportionality relationships are of the form $y = \dfrac{k}{x}$, where x is the input value and y is the output value. k is called the **proportionality constant**. This equation can also be written as $xy = k$, which means that the product of the output and input values is always constant.

For inverse proportionality problems, set up products for the "before" case and the "after" case, and then set the products equal to each other.

As with other proportion problems, you will typically be given "before" and "after" values. However, this time you set up **products**, not ratios, to solve the problem—for example, $y_1 x_1$ can be used for the "before" values and $y_2 x_2$ can be used for the "after" values. Next, we write $y_1 x_1 = y_2 x_2$, since each product equals the same constant k. Finally, we use algebra to solve for the unknowns in the problem.

> The amount of electrical current that flows through a wire is inversely proportional to the resistance in that wire. If a wire currently carries 4 amperes of electrical current, but the resistance is then cut to one-third of its original value, how many amperes of electrical current will flow through the wire?

While we are not given precise amounts for the "before" or "after" resistance in the wire, we can pick numbers. Using 3 as the original resistance and 1 as the new resistance, we can see that the new electrical current will be 12 amperes:

$$C_1 R_1 = C_2 R_2 \qquad\qquad 4(3) = C_2(1) \qquad\qquad 12 = C_2$$

LINEAR GROWTH

Many GMAT problems, especially word problems, feature quantities with **linear growth** (or decay)—that is, they grow at a constant rate. Such quantities are determined by the linear function: $y = mx + b$. In this equation, the slope m is the constant rate at which the quantity grows. The y-intercept b is the value of the quantity at time zero, and the variable (in this case, x) stands for time. You can also use t to represent time.

For instance, if a baby weighs 9 pounds at birth and gains 1.2 pounds per month, then the baby's weight can be written as $W = 9 + 1.2t$, where t is the baby's age in months. Note that $t = 0$ represents the birth of the baby.

> Jake was 4½ feet tall on his 12th birthday, when he began to have a growth spurt. Between his 12th and 15th birthdays, he grew at a constant rate. If Jake was 20% taller on his 15th birthday than on his 13th birthday, how many inches per year did Jake grow during his growth spurt? (12 inches = 1 foot)

In this problem, the constant growth does not begin until Jake has reached his twelfth birthday, so in order to use the constant growth function $y = mx + b$, let time $x = 0$ (the initial state) stand for Jake's twelfth birthday. Therefore, $x = 1$ stands for his 13th birthday, $x = 2$ stands for his 14th birthday, and $x = 3$ stands for his 15th birthday.

The problem asks for an answer in inches but gives you information in feet. Therefore, it is convenient to convert to inches at the beginning of the problem: 4½ feet = 54 inches = b. Since the growth rate m is unknown, the growth function can be written as $y = mx + 54$. Jake's height on his 13th birthday, when $x = 1$, was $54 + m$, and his height on his 15th birthday, when $x = 3$, was $54 + 3m$, which is 20% more than $54 + m$. Thus, we have:

$$54 + 3m = (54 + m) + 0.20(54 + m) \qquad 1.8m = 10.8$$
$$54 + 3m = 1.2(54 + m) \qquad\qquad\qquad m = 6$$
$$54 + 3m = 64.8 + 1.2m$$

Therefore, Jake grew at a rate of 6 inches each year.

For a problem involving linear growth, set up the equation $y = mx + b$.

Problem Set

1.   If $f(x) = 2x^4 - x^2$, what is the value of $f\left(2\sqrt{3}\right)$?

2.   If $g(x) = 3x + \sqrt{x}$, what is the value of $g(d^2 + 6d + 9)$?

3.   If $k(x) = 4x^3a$, and $k(3) = 27$, what is $k(2)$?

4.   If $f(x) = 3x - \sqrt{x}$ and $g(x) = x^2$, what is $f(g(4))$?

5.   If $f(x) = 3x - \sqrt{x}$ and $g(x) = x^2$, what is $g(f(4))$?

6.   If $f(x) = 2x^2 - 4$ and $g(x) = 2x$, for what values of x will $f(x) = g(x)$?

7.   If $f(x) = (x + \sqrt{3})^4$, what is the range of the function $f(x)$?
     (A) $\sqrt{3} < f(x) < 4$ (B) $f(x) \geq 0$ (C) $f(x) < 0$ (D) $f(x) \neq 0$

8.   If $g(x) = \dfrac{x^3 - ax}{4}$, and $g(2) = \dfrac{1}{2}$, what is the value of $g(4)$?

For problems #9–12, match each function with its graph.

9. $f(x) = -x^2 + 5$

10. $g(x) = |x - 1| - 1$

11. $h(x) = \dfrac{x}{3} + 4$

12. $k(x) = x^3$

(A)   (B)   (C)   (D)

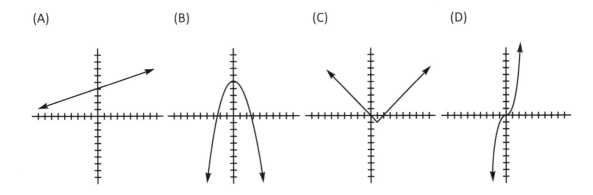

13.   The velocity of a falling object in a vacuum is directly proportional to the amount of time the object has been falling. If after 5 seconds an object is falling at a speed of 90 miles per hour, how fast will it be falling after 12 seconds?

14.   The "luminous flux," or perceived brightness, of a light source is measured in lumens and is inversely proportional to the square of the distance from the light. If a light source produces 200 lumens at a distance of 3 meters, at what distance will the light source produce a luminous flux of 25 lumens?

15.   If the function Q is defined by the formula $Q = \dfrac{5w}{4xz^2}$, by what factor will Q be multiplied if w is quadrupled, x is doubled, and z is tripled?

1. **276:** $f(x) = 2\left(2\sqrt{3}\right)^4 - \left(2\sqrt{3}\right)^2 = 2(2)^4\left(\sqrt{3}\right)^4 - (2)^2\left(\sqrt{3}\right)^2$

$$= (2 \cdot 16 \cdot 9) - (4 \cdot 3)$$
$$= 288 - 12 = 276$$

2. $\mathbf{3d^2 + 19d + 30}$ **OR** $\mathbf{3d^2 + 17d + 24}$**:**

$g(d^2 + 6d + 9) = 3(d^2 + 6d + 9) + \sqrt{d^2 + 6d + 9}$
$\qquad = 3d^2 + 18d + 27 + \sqrt{(d+3)^2}$
$\qquad = 3d^2 + 18d + 27 + d + 3 \qquad$ OR $\qquad 3d^2 + 18d + 27 - (d + 3)$
$\qquad = 3d^2 + 19d + 30 \qquad\qquad$ OR $\qquad 3d^2 + 17d + 24$
$\qquad$ (if $d + 3 \geq 0$) $\qquad\qquad\qquad\qquad$ (if $d + 3 \leq 0$)

3. **8:** $k(3) = 27$ Therefore,

$$4(3)^3 a = 27 \quad \rightarrow \quad k(x) = 4x^3\left(\frac{1}{4}\right) = x^3 \quad \rightarrow \quad k(2) = (2)^3 = 8$$

$$108a = 27$$

$$a = \frac{1}{4}$$

4. **44:** First, find the output value of the inner function: $g(4) = 16$.
Then, find $f(16)$: $3(16) - \sqrt{16} = 48 - 4 = 44$.

5. **100:** First, find the output value of the inner function: $f(4) = 3(4) - \sqrt{4} = 12 - 2 = 10$.
Then, find $g(10)$: $10^2 = 100$.

6. $\boldsymbol{x = \{-1, 2\}}$**:** To find the values for which $f(x) = g(x)$, set the functions equal to each other.

$$2x^2 - 4 = 2x$$
$$2x^2 - 2x - 4 = 0$$
$$2(x^2 - x - 2) = 0$$
$$2(x - 2)(x + 1) = 0$$

$$x - 2 = 0 \qquad \text{OR} \qquad x + 1 = 0$$
$$x = 2 \qquad\qquad\qquad\quad x = -1$$

7. **(B):** If $f(x) = (x + \sqrt{3})^4$, the range of outputs, or y-values, can never be negative. Regardless of the value of x, raising $x + \sqrt{3}$ to an even power will result in a non-negative y-value. Therefore, the range of the function is all non-negative numbers, or $f(x) \geq 0$.

8. **13:** $g(2) = \dfrac{(2)^3 - a(2)}{4} = \dfrac{1}{2}$

$$8 - 2a = 2$$

$$2a = 6 \quad \rightarrow \quad g(x) = \frac{x^3 - 3x}{4} \quad \rightarrow \quad g(4) = \frac{(4)^3 - 3(4)}{4} = \frac{64 - 12}{4} = 13$$

$$a = 3$$

9. **(B):** $f(x) = -x^2 + 5$. This function is a parabola. You can identify the correct graph by plotting the y-intercept $(0, 5)$.

10. **(C):** $g(x) = |x - 1| - 1$. This function is a V-shape. You can identify the correct graph by plotting the y-intercept $(0, 0)$ and then trying $x = 1$, which yields $y = -1$ and the point $(1, -1)$. These two points fall on the V-shape.

11. **(A):** $h(x) = \dfrac{x}{3} + 4$. This function is a straight line. You can identify the correct graph by plotting the y-intercept $(0, 4)$.

12. **(D):** $k(x) = x^3$. This is called a "cubic function." You can identify the correct graph by plotting the y-intercept $(0, 0)$ and then trying small positive and negative integers for x. If $x = 1$, $y = 1$; if $x = 2$, $y = 8$; if $x = -1$, $y = -1$; and if $x = -2$, $y = -8$. These numbers, when plotted, fit the cubic graph.

13. **216 miles per hour:** Because the velocity and the time spent falling are directly proportional, we can simply set the ratio of the "before" velocity and time to the "after" velocity and time:

$$\frac{v_1}{w_1} = \frac{v_2}{w_2}$$

$$\frac{90\,\text{mph}}{5\,\text{sec}} = \frac{v_2}{12\,\text{sec}}$$

$$v_2 = \frac{90(12)}{5} = 216\,\text{mph}$$

14. **$6\sqrt{2}$ meters:** Because the intensity of the light source and the SQUARE of the distance are inversely proportional, we can write the product of the "before" intensity and distance squared and the product of the "after" intensity and distance squared. Then we set these two products equal to each other:

$$I_1 \cdot d_1^2 = I_2 \cdot d_2^2$$

$$(200\,\text{lumens}) \cdot (3\,\text{meters})^2 = (25\,\text{lumens}) \cdot d_2^2$$

$$d_2^2 = \frac{(200\,\text{lumens}) \cdot (3\,\text{meters})^2}{(25\,\text{lumens})} = 8(3^2) = 72$$

$$d_2 = 6\sqrt{2}\,\text{meters}$$

15. $\dfrac{2}{9}$: The formula shows that Q is directly proportional to w and inversely proportional to x and to z^2. Therefore, Q will change by the same factor as does w, and it will change by factors that are the RECIP-ROCALS of the factors by which x and z^2 change. Quadrupling w will multiply Q by 4. Doubling x will cut Q in half (multiply Q by $\dfrac{1}{2}$). Tripling z causes z^2 to increase by a factor of 9, which will multiply Q by $\dfrac{1}{9}$. Therefore, Q will be multiplied overall by a factor of $4 \times \dfrac{1}{2} \times \dfrac{1}{9} = \dfrac{2}{9}$.

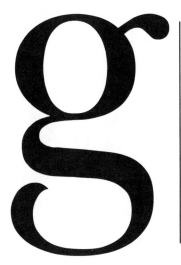

Chapter 6
of
EQUATIONS, INEQUALITIES, & VICs

INEQUALITIES

In This Chapter . . .

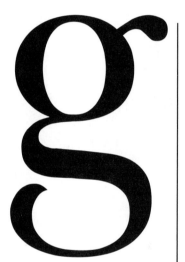

INEQUALITIES

Unlike equations, which relate two equivalent quantities, inequalities compare quantities that have different values. Inequalities are used to express four kinds of relationships, illustrated by the following examples.

(1) x is less than 4

$x < 4$

(2) x is less than or equal to 4

$x \leq 4$

(3) x is greater than 4

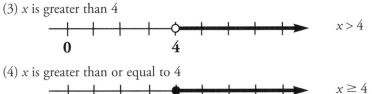

$x > 4$

(4) x is greater than or equal to 4

$x \geq 4$

Number lines, such as those shown above, are an excellent way to visualize exactly what a given inequality means.

Much Like Equations, With One Big Exception

Many operations that can be performed on equations can be performed on inequalities. For example, in order to simplify an expression (e.g. $2 + x < 5$), you can **add or subtract a constant on both sides:**

$$
\begin{array}{r}
2 + x < 5 \\
-2 \quad\quad -2 \\
\hline
x < 3
\end{array}
\qquad
\begin{array}{r}
x - 5 < 9 \\
+5 \quad +5 \\
\hline
x \quad\quad < 14
\end{array}
$$

You can also **add or subtract a variable expression on both sides:**

$$
\begin{array}{r}
y + x < 5 \\
-y \quad\quad\quad -y \\
\hline
x < 5 - y
\end{array}
\qquad
\begin{array}{r}
x - ab < 9 \\
+ab \quad\quad +ab \\
\hline
x \quad\quad < 9 + ab
\end{array}
$$

You can **multiply or divide by a <u>positive</u> number on both sides:**

$$
\begin{array}{r}
2x < 6 \\
\div 2 \quad \div 2 \\
\hline
x < 3
\end{array}
\qquad
\begin{array}{r}
0.2x < 1 \\
\times 5 \quad \times 5 \\
\hline
x < 5
\end{array}
$$

Manhattan **GMAT** Prep

the new standard

Inequalities specify a range on the number line, but be mindful of whether the endpoint is included in the range.

There is, however, one procedure that makes inequalities different from equations: **When you multiply or divide an inequality by a negative number, the inequality sign flips!**

Given that $4 - 3x < 10$, what is the range of possible values for x?

$$4 - 3x < 10$$
$$\underline{-4 \qquad -4}$$
$$-3x < 6$$
$$\underline{\div(-3) \quad \div(-3)}$$
$$x > -2$$

In isolating x in this equation, we divide both sides by -3. Because we divide by a negative number, the inequality sign flips from **less than** to **greater than**!

A corollary of this is that **you cannot multiply or divide an inequality by a variable, unless you know the sign of the number that the variable stands for**. The reason is that you would not know whether to flip the inequality sign.

> When you multiply or divide by a negative number or variable, you must flip the sign of the inequality.

Combining Inequalities: Line 'Em Up!

Many GMAT inequality problems involve more than one inequality. To solve such problems, you may need to convert several inequalities to a **compound inequality**, which is a series of inequalities strung together, such as $2 < 3 < 4$. To convert multiple inequalities to a compound inequality, first line up the variables, then combine.

If $x > 8$, $x < 17$, and $x + 5 < 19$, what is the range of possible values for x?

First, solve any inequalities that need to be solved. In this example, only the last inequality needs to be solved.

$$x + 5 < 19$$
$$x < 14$$

Second, simplify the inequalities so that all the inequality symbols point in the same direction, preferably to the left (less than).

$$8 < x$$
$$x < 17$$
$$x < 14$$

Third, line up the common variables in the inequalities.

$$8 < x$$
$$x < 17$$
$$x < 14$$

Finally, combine the inequalities by taking the more limiting upper and lower extremes.

$$8 < x < 14$$

Notice that $x < 14$ is more limiting than $x < 17$ (in other words, whenever $x < 14$, x will always be less than 17, but not vice versa.) That is why we choose $8 < x < 14$ rather than $8 < x < 17$ as the compound inequality that solves the problem. We simply discard the less limiting inequality, $x < 17$.

Given that $u < t$, $b > r$, $f < t$, and $r > t$, is $b > u$?

Combine the 4 given inequalities by simplifying and lining up the common variables.

Simplify the list: $u < t$, $r < b$, $f < t$, and $t < r$.

Then, line up the variables...   ...and combine.

$u < t$ $u < t < r < b$
$\quad\quad r < b$ $f < t$
$f < t$
$\quad t < r$

> Line up multiple inequalities to see whether they can be combined into a compound inequality, which may be helpful in solving the problem.

When working with multiple variables, it is not always possible to combine all the inequalities, as we see in this example. We cannot really fit the inequality $f < t$ into the long combination. We do know that both u and f are less than t, but we do not know the relationship between u and f.

We can see from our combination that the answer to the question is YES: b is greater than u.

Manipulating Compound Inequalities

Sometimes a problem with compound inequalities will require you to manipulate the inequalities in order to solve the problem. You can perform operations on a compound inequality as long as you remember to perform those operations on **every term** in the inequality, not just the outside terms. For example:

$x + 3 < y < x + 5 \longrightarrow x < y < x + 2$ **WRONG**: you must subtract 3 from EVERY term in the inequality

$x + 3 < y < x + 5 \longrightarrow x < y - 3 < x + 2$ CORRECT

$\dfrac{c}{2} \leq b - 3 \leq \dfrac{d}{2} \longrightarrow c \leq b - 3 \leq d$ **WRONG**: you must multiply by 2 in EVERY term in the inequality

$\dfrac{c}{2} \leq b - 3 \leq \dfrac{d}{2} \longrightarrow c \leq 2b - 6 \leq d$ CORRECT

If $1 > 1 - ab > 0$, which of the following must be true?

I. $\dfrac{a}{b} > 0$

II. $\dfrac{a}{b} < 1$

III. $ab < 1$

(A) I only
(B) II only
(C) III only
(D) I and II only
(E) I and III only

When you manipulate
compound inequalities,
be sure to manipulate
every term in exactly the
same way.

We can manipulate the original compound inequality as follows, making sure to perform each manipulation on every term:

$$1 > 1 - ab > 0$$
$$0 > \quad -ab > -1 \qquad \text{Subtract 1 from all three terms}$$
$$0 < \quad ab < 1 \qquad \text{Multiply all three terms by } -1 \text{ and flip the inequality signs}$$

Therefore we know that $0 < ab < 1$. This tells us that ab is positive, so $\dfrac{a}{b}$ must be positive (a and b have the same sign). Therefore, I must be true. However, we do not know whether $\dfrac{a}{b} < 1$, so II is not necessarily true. But we do know that ab must be less than 1, so III must be true. Therefore, the correct answer is **(E)**.

Combining Inequalities: Add 'Em Up!

As discussed above, many GMAT inequality problems involve more than one inequality. Another helpful approach is to combine inequalities by **adding the inequalities together**. In order to add inequalities, we must make sure the inequality signs are facing the same direction.

Is $a + 2b < c + 2d$?

(1) $a < c$
(2) $d > b$

For this problem, we can add the inequalities together to make them match the question. First, we need to line up the inequalities so that they are all facing the same direction:

$$a < c$$
$$b < d$$

Then we can take the sum of the two inequalities to prove the result. We will need to add the second inequality TWICE:

$$
\begin{array}{r}
a \qquad < c \\
+ \quad b < \qquad d \\
\hline
a + b < c + d \\
+ \quad b < \qquad d \\
\hline
a + 2b < c + 2d
\end{array}
$$

If you use both statements, you can answer the question. Therefore the answer is **(C)**.

Notice that we also could have multiplied the second inequality by 2 before summing, so that the result matched the original question:

$$
\begin{array}{r}
a \qquad < c \\
+ \quad 2(b < \qquad d) \\
\hline
a + 2b < c + 2d
\end{array}
$$

You can add inequalities together as long as the inequality signs are pointing in the same direction.

Adding inequalities together is a powerful technique on the GMAT. However, note that we should never subtract or divide two inequalities. Moreover, you can only multiply inequalities together under certain circumstances.

> Is $mn < 10$?
>
> (1) $m < 2$
> (2) $n < 5$

It is tempting to multiply these two statements together and conclude that $mn < 10$. That would be a mistake, however, because both m and n could be negative numbers that yield a number larger than 10 when multiplied together. For example, if $m = -2$ and $n = -6$, then $mn = 12$, which is greater than 10.

Since you can find cases with $mn < 10$ and cases with $mn > 10$, the correct answer is **(E)**: The two statements together are INSUFFICIENT to answer the question definitively.

Now consider this variation:

> If m and n are both positive, is $mn < 10$?
>
> (1) $m < 2$
>
> (2) $n < 5$

Since the variables are positive, we <u>can</u> multiply these inequalities together and conclude that $mn < 10$. The correct answer is (C).

Only multiply inequalities together if both sides of both inequalities are positive.

Using Extreme Values

One effective technique for solving GMAT inequality problems is to focus on the EXTREME VALUES of a given inequality. This is particularly helpful when solving the following types of inequality problems:

(1) Problems with multiple inequalities where the question involves the potential range of values for variables in the problem
(2) Problems involving both equations and inequalities

INEQUALITIES WITH RANGES

Whenever a question asks about the possible range of values for a problem, consider using extreme values:

Plug extreme values using "LT" for "less than" or "GT" for "greater than."

> Given that $0 \leq x \leq 3$, and $y < 8$, which of the following could NOT be the value of xy?
>
> (A) 0   (B) 8   (C) 12   (D) 16   (E) 24

To solve this problem, consider the EXTREME VALUES of each variable.

Extreme Values for x	Extreme Values for y
The lowest value for x is **0**.	There is no lower limit to y.
The highest value for x is **3**.	The highest value for y is **less than 8**.

(Since y cannot be 8, we term this upper limit "less than 8" or "LT8" for shorthand.)

What is the lowest value for xy? Plug in the lowest values for both x and y. In this problem, y has no lower limit, so there is no lower limit to xy.

What is the highest value for xy? Plug in the highest values for both x and y. In this problem, the highest value for x is **3**, and the highest value for y is **LT8**.

Multiplying these two extremes together yields: $3 \times$ LT8 = LT24. Notice that we can multiply LT8 by another number (as long as that other number is positive) just as though it were 8. We just have to remember to include the "LT" tag on the result.

Because the upper extreme for xy is less than 24, xy CANNOT be 24, and the answer is (E).

Notice that we would run into trouble if x did not have to be non-negative. Consider this slight variation:

> Given that $-1 \leq x \leq 3$, and $y < 8$, what is the possible range of values for xy?

Because x could be negative and because y could be a large negative number, there is no longer an upper extreme on xy. For example, if $x = -1$ and $y = -1,000$, then $xy = 1,000$. Obviously, much larger results are possible for xy if both x and y are negative. Therefore, xy can equal any number.

INEQUALITIES WITH EQUATIONS

Whenever a problem contains both inequalities and equations, extreme values can help you substitute values from one to the other:

> If $2h + k < 8$, $g + 3h = 15$, and $k = 4$, what is the possible range of values for g?

First, we can simplify the inequality by plugging 4 in for k to simplify the inequality:

$$2h + 4 < 8 \qquad 2h < 4 \qquad h < 2$$

Now, we can use extreme values to combine the inequality with the equation. If we think of $h < 2$ in terms of extreme values, then $h = LT2$. We can plug this extreme value into the equation and solve for g:

Extreme values provide an efficient way to solve problems involving both inequalities and equations.

$$g + 3h = 15 \qquad\qquad g = 15 - LT6$$
$$g + 3(LT2) = 15 \qquad\qquad g = GT(9)$$
$$g + LT6 = 15 \qquad\qquad g > 9$$

Notice that when we subtract LT6 from 15, we have to CHANGE the extreme value sign from LT to GT. Think of it this way: if we subtract 6 from 15, the result is 9. But if we subtract a number SMALLER than 6 from 15, the result will be LARGER than 9.

Alternatively, you could solve for h in the equation in this problem, plug the result in for h in the inequality, and simplify to arrive at the same solution:

$$g + 3h = 15$$
$$3h = 15 - g$$
$$h = \frac{15 - g}{3} = 5 - \frac{g}{3}$$
$$2\left(5 - \frac{g}{3}\right) + k < 8$$
$$2\left(5 - \frac{g}{3}\right) + 4 < 8$$

$$2\left(5 - \frac{g}{3}\right) < 4$$
$$10 - \frac{2g}{3} < 4$$
$$-\frac{2g}{3} < -6$$
$$g > 9$$

Notice that this "standard algebra" approach (solve the equation first, then substitute into the inequality) is less efficient in this case. You should know how to solve problems involving inequalities and equations both ways: (1) plug the inequality into the equation using extreme values, and (2) plug the equation into the inequality using standard algebra. Moreover, you should assess which one is more efficient for any given problem.

The following table summarizes many of the mathemetical operations you can perform using extreme values.

SAMPLE EXTREME VALUES OPERATIONS

Operation	Example	Procedure
Addition	8 + LT2	Add just like regular numbers: 8 + LT2 = LT10 (i.e., < 10)
Subtraction	8 − LT2	Subtract and flip the extreme value: 8 − LT2 = GT6 (i.e., > 6)
Multiplication	a) 8 × LT2 b) −7 × LT2	a) Multiply just like regular numbers: 8 × LT2 = LT16 (i.e., < 16) b) Multiply and flip the extreme value: −7 × LT2 = GT(−14) (i.e., > −14)
Division	8 ÷ LT2	Divide and flip the extreme value: 8 ÷ LT2 = GT4 (i.e., > 4) if we know that LT2 is positive
Multiply two extreme values	LT8 × LT2	Multiply just like regular numbers: LT8 × LT2 = LT16 (i.e., < 16) if we know that both extreme values are positive

Pay close attention to how arithmetic operations affect extreme values.

Optimization Problems

Related to extreme values are problems involving optimization: specifically, minimization or maximization problems. In these problems, you need to **focus on the largest and smallest possible values for each of the variables**, as some combination of them will usually lead to the largest or smallest possible result.

> If $2y + 3 \leq 11$ and $1 \leq x \leq 5$, what is the maximum possible value for xy?

We need to test the extreme values for x and for y to determine which combinations of extreme values will maximize xy:

$$2y + 3 \leq 11 \qquad\qquad 2y \leq 8 \qquad\qquad y \leq 4$$

Extreme Values for x	**Extreme Values for y**
The lowest value for x is 1.	There is no lower limit to y.
The highest value for x is 5.	The highest value for y is 4.

Now let us consider the different extreme value scenarios for x, y, and xy:

Since y has no lower limit and x is positive, the product xy has no lower limit.

Using y's highest value (4), we test the extreme values of x (1 and 5). The first extreme value generates a product $xy = (1)(4) = 4$. The second extreme value generates $xy = (5)(4) = 20$.

Clearly, xy is maximized when $x = 5$ and $y = 4$, with a result that $xy = 20$.

*Manhattan***GMAT** *Prep
the new standard

If $-7 \leq a \leq 6$ and $-7 \leq b \leq 8$, what is the maximum possible value for ab?

Once again, we are looking for a maximum possible value, this time for ab. We need to test the extreme values for a and for b to determine which combinations of extreme values will maximize ab:

Extreme Values for _a_	**Extreme Values for _b_**
The lowest value for a is -7.	The lowest value for b is -7.
The highest value for a is 6.	The highest value for b is 8.

Now let us consider the different extreme value scenarios for a, b, and ab:

	a		b	ab
Min	-7	Min	-7	$(-7) \times (-7) = \mathbf{49}$
Min	-7	Max	8	$(-7) \times 8 = -56$
Max	6	Min	-7	$6 \times (-7) = -42$
Max	6	Max	8	$6 \times 8 = 48$

This time, ab is maximized when we take the NEGATIVE extreme values for both a and b, resulting in $ab = 49$. Notice that we could have focused right away on the first and fourth scenarios, because they are the only scenarios which produce positive products.

If $-4 \leq m \leq 7$ and $-3 < n < 10$, what is the maximum possible integer value for $m - n$?

Again, we are looking for a maximum possible value, this time for $m - n$. We need to test the extreme values for m and for n to determine which combinations of extreme values will maximize $m - n$:

Extreme Values for _m_	**Extreme Values for _n_**
The lowest value for m is -4.	The lowest value for n is greater than -3.
The highest value for m is 7.	The highest value for n is less than 10.

Now let us consider the different extreme value scenarios for m, n, and $m - n$:

	m		n	$m - n$
Min	-4	Min	GT(-3)	$(-4) - \text{GT}(-3) = \text{LT}(-1)$
Min	-4	Max	LT10	$(-4) - \text{LT}10 = \text{GT}(-14)$
Max	7	Min	**GT(-3)**	$\mathbf{7 - GT(-3) = LT10}$
Max	7	Max	LT10	$7 - \text{LT}10 = \text{GT}(-3)$

$m - n$ is maximized when we take the POSITIVE extreme for m and the NEGATIVE extreme for n, resulting in $m - n = $ LESS THAN 10. The largest integer less than 10 is 9, so the correct answer is $m - n = 9$.

*Manhattan*GMAT®Prep

the new standard

For maximization and minimization problems, check the endpoints of the ranges for each variable.

If $x \geq 4 + (z + 1)^2$, what is the minimum possible value for x?

As we saw in the Functions chapter, the key to this type of problem—where we need to maximize or minimize when one of the variables has an even exponent—is to recognize that the squared term will be minimized when it is set equal to zero. Therefore, we need to set $(z + 1)^2$ equal to 0:

$$(z + 1)^2 = 0$$
$$z + 1 = 0$$
$$z = -1$$

The smallest square is zero. This fact can unlock certain optimization problems.

The minimum possible value for x occurs when $z = -1$, and $x \geq 4 + (-1 + 1)^2 = 4 + 0 = 4$. Therefore $\boldsymbol{x \geq 4}$, so 4 is the minimum possible value for x.

Testing Inequality Cases

So far we have seen several examples in which we have to consider different cases, or scenarios, for values and then determine what implications those scenarios have for the problem.

There are other common situations in which you need to consider multiple cases. Specifically, inequalities problems frequently involve testing POSITIVE or NEGATIVE CASES for the variables involved.

Is $d > 0$?

(1) $bc < 0$
(2) $cd > 0$

Clearly, Statement (1) is insufficient to answer the question, as it tells us nothing about d. Statement (2) is insufficient, because either c and d are both positive, or c and d are both negative. Therefore, we only need to test the positive/negative cases that fit Statements (1) and (2) together. That occurs when b and c have different signs, while c and d have the same sign:

b	c	d	$bc < 0$?	$cd > 0$?
+	−	−	YES	YES
−	+	+	YES	YES

It is possible that EITHER b is positive and both c and d are negative, OR b is negative and both c and d are positive. Since d could be either positive or negative, the correct answer is **(E)**: The two statements together are INSUFFICIENT to answer the question definitively.

Is $bd < 0$?

(1) $bc < 0$
(2) $cd > 0$

Notice that this problem is the same as the previous one, except that the question has changed. Clearly, Statement (1) is insufficient to answer the question, as it tells us nothing about d. Statement (2) is insufficient, because it tells us nothing about b. Therefore, we only need to test the positive/negative cases that fit Statements (1) and (2) together. That occurs when b and c have different signs, while c and d have the same sign:

b	c	d	$bc < 0$?	$cd > 0$?	bd?
$+$	$-$	$-$	YES	YES	$-$
$-$	$+$	$+$	YES	YES	$-$

Use positive/negative rules to set up scenarios for many inequality problems.

Either way, b and d have opposite signs, so $bd < 0$. The correct answer is **(C)**: Together the statments are SUFFICIENT to answer the question definitively.

Here are some common inequality statements on the GMAT, as well as what they imply. You should think of these translations whenever you see one of these statements on the test:

STATEMENT	IMPLICATION
$xy > 0$	x and y are <u>both positive</u> OR <u>both negative</u>
$xy < 0$	x and y have <u>different signs</u> (one positive, one negative)
$x^2 - x < 0$	$x^2 < x$, so <u>$0 < x < 1$</u>

When you see inequalities **with zero on one side of the inequality**, you should **consider using positive/negative analysis** to help solve the problem!

Inequalities and Absolute Value

Absolute value can be a confusing concept—particularly in a problem involving inequalities. For these types of problems, it is often helpful to try to visualize the problem with a number line.

For a simple equation such as $|x| = 5$, the graph of the solutions looks like this:

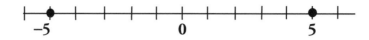

When absolute value is used in an inequality, the unknown generally has more than two possible solutions. Indeed, for a simple inequality such as $|x| < 5$, the graph of the solutions covers a range:

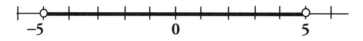

One way to understand this inequality is to say "x must be less than 5 units from zero on the number line." Indeed, **one interpretation of absolute value is simply distance on the number line**. For a simple absolute value expression such as $|x|$, we are evaluating distance from zero.

Absolute values can be more difficult to graph than the one above. Consider, for instance, the inequality $|x + 2| < 5$. This seems more difficult, because the "+ 2" term seems to throw a wrench into our distance-on-the-number-line interpretation of this problem.

However, there is a relatively straightforward way to think about this problem. First, create a number line for the term inside the absolute value bars. Here, we create a number line for "$x + 2$." We can see that this expression as a whole must be between -5 and 5:

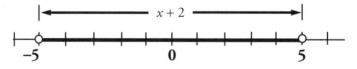

In other words, $x + 2$ must be less than 5 units away from zero on the number line. We can not stop there—we must graph for x alone. How does the "+ 2" change our graph? It forces us to shift the entire graph down by 2, because the absolute value expression will be equal to zero when $x = -2$. Thus, the graph for x alone will look like this:

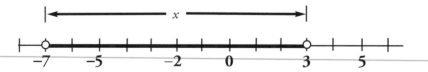

Notice that the center point for the possible values of x is now -2, which is the value for x that fits $x + 2 = 0$. This is the "center point" for the number line graph. The distance from the center point (-2) to either end point remains the same.

From this example, we can extract a standard formula for interpreting absolute value. When $|x + b| = c$, the center point of our graph is $-b$. The equation tells us that x must be EXACTLY c units away from $-b$. Similarly, for the inequality $|x + b| < c$, the center point of the graph is $-b$, and the "less than" symbol tells us that x must be LESS THAN c units away from $-b$.

> What is the graph of $|x - 4| < 3$?

Based on this formula, the center point of the graph is $-(-4) = 4$, and x must be less than 3 units away from that point:

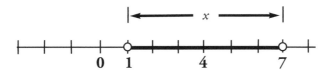

We can also solve these types of problems algebraically. Recall that equations involving absolute value require you to consider **two** scenarios: one where the expression inside the absolute value brackets is positive, and one where the expression is negative. The same is true for inequalities. For example:

> Given that $|x - 2| < 5$, what is the range of possible values for x?

To work out the FIRST scenario, we simply remove the absolute value brackets and solve.

$$|x - 2| < 5 \qquad\qquad x - 2 < 5 \qquad\qquad x < 7$$

To work out the SECOND scenario, we reverse the signs of the terms inside the absolute value brackets, remove the brackets, and solve again.

$$\begin{aligned} |x - 2| &< 5 \\ -(x - 2) &< 5 \\ -x + 2 &< 5 \end{aligned} \qquad\qquad \begin{aligned} -x &< 3 \\ x &> -3 \end{aligned}$$

We can combine these two scenarios into one range of values for x: $-3 < x < 7$. This range is illustrated by the following number line:

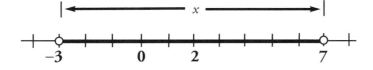

Note that this range fits in perfectly with our number-line interpretation of absolute value: this graph is the set of all points such that x is less than 5 units away from $-(-2) = 2$.

As an aside, note also that you should **never** change $|x - 5|$ to $x + 5$. This is a common mistake. Remember, when you drop the absolute value signs, you either leave the expression alone or enclose the ENTIRE expression in parentheses and put a negative sign in front.

Many absolute value inequality problems can be solved either by drawing the acceptable range on the number line, or by using algebra.

Square-Rooting Inequalities

Just like equations involving even exponents, inequality problems involving even exponents require you to consider **two** scenarios. Consider this example:

> If $x^2 < 4$, what are the possible values for x?

To solve this problem, recall that $\sqrt{x^2} = |x|$. For example, $\sqrt{3^2} = 3$, and $\sqrt{(-5)^2} = 5$. Therefore, when we take the square root of both sides of the inequality, we get:

$$\sqrt{x^2} < \sqrt{4}$$
$$|x| < 2$$

When you take the square root of an inequality, you will often need to evaluate an absolute value scenario.

If x is positive, then $x < 2$. On the other hand, if x is negative, then $x > -2$. Alternatively, we can just think of the problem as we did in the previous section: x must be less than 2 units away from 0 on the number line.

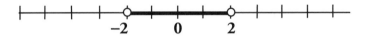

Here is another example:

> If $10 + x^2 \geq 19$, what is the range of possible values for x?

$$10 + x^2 \geq 19$$
$$x^2 \geq 9$$
$$|x| \geq 3$$

If x is positive, then $x \geq 3$. If x is negative, then $x \leq -3$. Alternatively, we can just think of the problem as we did in the previous section: x must be MORE THAN (or exactly) 3 units away from 0 on the number line.

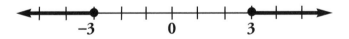

Note that you can ONLY take the square root of an inequality for which both sides are definitely NOT negative, since you cannot take the square root of a negative number. Restrict this technique to situations in which the square of a variable or expression must be positive.

Summary of Inequality Techniques

We have covered many topics in inequalities. Here is a quick recap of "DOs and DON'Ts" when working with inequalities:

DOs	DON'Ts
• DO think about inequalities as ranges on a number line.	• DON'T forget to flip the inequality sign if you multiply or divide both sides of an inequality by a negative number.
• DO treat inequalities like equations when adding or subtracting terms, or when multiplying/dividing by a positive number on both sides of the inequality.	• DON'T multiply or divide an inequality by a variable unless you know the sign of the variable.
• DO line up multiple inequalities to form a compound inequality when doing so may help solve to the problem.	• DON'T forget to take the most restrictive inequality when dealing with multiple inequalities involving the same variable (for example, $x < 0$ and $x < -1$ means that $x < -1$).
• DO add inequalities together when doing so may help solve to the problem.	
• DO use extreme values to solve inequality range problems, problems containing both inequalities and equations, and many optimization problems.	• DON'T forget to perform operations on every expression when manipulating a compound inequality.
• DO set terms with even exponents equal to zero when trying to solve optimization problems.	• DON'T subtract one inequality from another. Do not multiply together inequalities unless all the expressions are positive.
• DO draw a number line to think through inequality problems involving absolute value or even exponents.	• DON'T forget that many positive/negative problems are disguised as inequality problems.
	• DON'T forget about the negative case when solving inequality problems that contain even exponents.

Memorize the list of things you can— and cannot—do when manipulating inequalities.

*Manhattan*GMAT*Prep
the new standard

Problem Set

1.   If $4x - 12 \geq x + 9$, which of the following must be true?
     (A) $x > 6$ (B) $x < 7$ (C) $x > 7$ (D) $x > 8$ (E) $x < 8$

2.   Which of the following is equivalent to $-3x + 7 \leq 2x + 32$?
     (A) $x \geq -5$ (B) $x \geq 5$ (C) $x \leq 5$ (D) $x \leq -5$

3.   If $G^2 < G$, which of the following could be G?

     (A) 1   (B) $\dfrac{23}{7}$ (C) $\dfrac{7}{23}$ (D) -4 (E) -2

4.   If $5B > 4B + 1$, is $B^2 > 1$?

5.   If $|A| > 19$, which of the following could not be equal to A?
     (A) 26   (B) 22   (C) 18   (D) -20 (E) -24

6.   If $|10y - 4| > 7$ and $y < 1$, which of the following could be y?
     (A) -0.8 (B) -0.1 (C) 0.1   (D) 0   (E) 1

7.   If $a > 7$, $a + 4 > 13$, and $2a < 30$, which of the following must be true?
     (A) $9 < a < 15$ (B) $11 < a < 15$ (C) $15 < a < 20$ (D) $13 < a < 15$

8.   If $d > a$ and $L < a$, which of the following cannot be true?
     (A) $d + L = 14$ (B) $d - L = 7$ (C) $d - L = 1$ (D) $a - d = 9$ (E) $a + d = 9$

9.   If $a^2 b > 1$ and $b < 2$, which of the following could be the value of a?

     (A) $\dfrac{1}{2}$ (B) $\dfrac{1}{4}$ (C) $-\dfrac{1}{2}$ (D) -2 (E) $\dfrac{2}{3}$

10. If $\dfrac{AB}{7} > \dfrac{1}{14}$ and $A = B$, which of the following must be greater than 1?

     (A) $A + B$ (B) $1 - A$ (C) $2A^2$ (D) $A^2 - \dfrac{1}{2}$ (E) A

11. If $B^3 A < 0$ and $A > 0$, which of the following must be negative?

     (A) AB (B) $B^2 A$ (C) B^4 (D) $\dfrac{A}{B^2}$ (E) $-\dfrac{B}{A}$

12. Graph each of the following expressions:
     (A) $|x| = 5$ (B) $|x| < 4$ (C) $|x - 4| = 3$ (D) $|x - 3| < 4$ (E) $|x + 5| \geq 2$

13. If $qp = 18$, $r = 2$, and $7 < p + 2r$, what is the range of possible values for q?

14. If x and y are integers such that $(x + 1)^2 \leq 36$ and $(y - 1)^2 < 64$, what is the largest possible value of xy ?

15. If $0 < ab < ac$, is a negative?
     (1) $c < 0$
     (2) $b > c$

1. **(A):** $4x - 12 \geq x + 9$
$\qquad 3x \geq 21$
$\qquad\quad x \geq 7$ If $x \geq 7$, then $x > 6$.

2. **(A):** $-3x + 7 \leq 2x + 32$
$\qquad\quad -5x \leq 25$ When you divide by a negative number, you must
$\qquad\qquad x \geq -5$ reverse the direction of the inequality symbol.

3. **(C):** IF $G^2 < G$, then G must be positive (since G^2 will never be negative), and G must be less than 1, because otherwise, $G^2 > G$. Thus, $0 < G < 1$. We can eliminate (D) and (E), since they violate the condition that G be positive. Then test (A): 1 is not less than 1, so we can eliminate (A). (B) is larger than 1, so only (C) satisfies the inequality.

4. **YES:** $5B > 4B + 1$
$\qquad\quad B > 1$
The squares of all numbers greater than 1 are also greater than 1. So $B^2 > 1$.

5. **(C):** If $\left| A \right| > 19$, then $A > 19$ OR $A < -19$. The only answer choice that does not satisfy either of these inequalities is (C), 18.

6. **(A):** First, eliminate any answer choices that do not satisfy the simpler of the two inequalities, $y < 1$. Based on this inequality alone, you can eliminate (E). Then, simplify the first inequality.

$$10y - 4 > 7 \qquad \text{OR} \qquad -10y + 4 > 7$$
$$10y > 11 \qquad\qquad\qquad 10y < -3$$
$$y > 1.1 \qquad\qquad\qquad\quad y < \frac{-3}{10}$$

The only answer choice that satisfies this inequality is (A) -0.8.

7. **(A):** First, solve the second and third inequalities. Simplify the inequalities, so that all the inequality symbols point in the same direction. Then, line up the inequalities as shown. Finally, combine the inequalities.

$$9 < a$$
$$\quad a < 15 \qquad\qquad \rightarrow \qquad\qquad 9 < a < 15$$
$$7 < a$$

Notice that all the wrong answers are more constrained: the low end is too high. The right answer will <u>both</u> keep out all the impossible values of a <u>and</u> let in all the possible values of a.

8. **(D):** Simplify the inequalities, so that all the inequality symbols point in the same direction. Then, line up the inequalities as shown. Finally, combine the inequalities.

$$L < a$$
$$a < d \qquad \rightarrow \qquad L < a < d$$

Since d is a larger number than a, $a - d$ cannot be positive. Therefore, (D) cannot be true.

9. **(D):** Note that because $a^2b > 1$, a^2b is positive, meaning that b must be positive. (Since b is positive, we do not have to worry about switching the inequality sign after dividing by b.) Plug the upper extreme value of b into the first inequality:

$$a^2(LT\,2) > 1 \qquad\qquad a^2 > GT\,\frac{1}{2}$$

$$a^2 > \frac{1}{LT\,2}$$

1 divided by a positive number less than 2 is greater than $\frac{1}{2}$.

(D) -2 is the only answer choice that, when squared, yields a number greater than $\frac{1}{2}$.

10. **(C):** $\dfrac{AB}{7} > \dfrac{1}{14}$

$14AB > 7$ Cross-multiply across the inequality.

$2AB > 1$ Then, divide both sides by 7.

$2A^2 > 1$ Since you know that $A = B$, $2AB = 2A^2$.

11. **(A):** If A is positive, B^3 must be negative. Therefore, B must be negative. If A is positive and B is negative, the product AB must be negative.

12. (A): $x = \{-5, 5\}$:

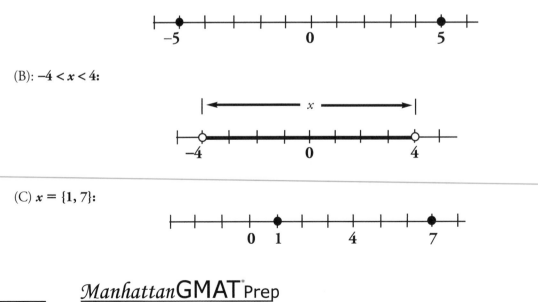

(B): $-4 < x < 4$:

(C) $x = \{1, 7\}$:

(D) $-1 < x < 7$:

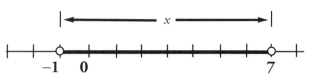

(E) $x \leq -7$ OR $x \geq -3$:

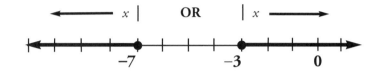

13. **$0 < q < 6$:** First, we can simplify the inequality by plugging 2 in for r to simplify the inequality:

$$7 < p + 2(2) \qquad\qquad 7 - 4 < p \qquad\qquad p > 3$$

Now, we can use extreme values to combine the inequality with the equation. If we think of $p > 3$ in terms of extreme values, then $p = GT3$. We can plug this extreme value into the equation and solve for q:

$$qp = 18 \qquad\qquad q = LT6$$
$$q(GT3) = 18 \qquad\qquad q < 6$$
$$q = \frac{18}{GT3}$$

Thus q must be less than 6. However, notice that p must be greater than 3, so p is positive. For qp to equal 18, q must also be positive. Therefore, $0 < q < 6$.

14. **42:** First, we need to determine the possible ranges for x and y:

$$(x + 1)^2 \leq 36 \qquad\qquad\qquad (y - 1)^2 < 64$$
$$\sqrt{(x+1)^2} \leq \sqrt{36} \qquad\qquad \sqrt{(y-1)^2} < \sqrt{64}$$
$$|x + 1| \leq 6 \qquad\qquad\qquad |y - 1| < 8$$
$$-7 \leq x \leq 5 \qquad\qquad\qquad -7 < y < 9$$

In order to maximize xy, we need to test the endpoints of the ranges for x and y. Notice that the smallest value for y is -6 and the largest value for y is 8, because y must be an integer:

If $x = -7$ and $y = -6$, $xy = 42$.
If $x = -7$ and $y = 8$, $xy = -56$.
If $x = 5$ and $y = -6$, $xy = -30$.
If $x = 5$ and $y = 8$, $xy = 40$.

Thus the maximum value for xy is 42.

15. **(D):** By the transitive property of inequalities, if $0 < ab < ac$, then $0 < ac$. Therefore a and c must have the same sign. Statement (1) tells us that c is negative. Therefore, a is negative. SUFFICIENT.

Statement (2) is trickier. Consider the fact that $ab < ac$. If we were to divide both sides of the inequality by a, we would have $b < c$ whenever a is positive and $b > c$ whenever a is negative (if a is negative, you would have to flip the sign when dividing by a). Because Statement (2) tells us that $b > c$, we know that a must be negative. SUFFICIENT.

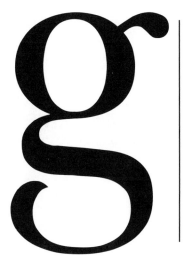

Chapter 7
of

EQUATIONS, INEQUALITIES, & VICs

VICs

In This Chapter . . .

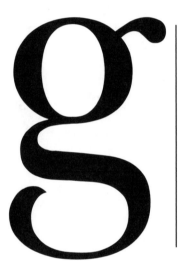

VIC PROBLEMS

One way the GMAT tests your ability to work with variables is through VIC problems. VIC problems are those that have **V**ARIABLE EXPRESSIONS **I**N THE ANSWER **C**HOICES.

A typical VIC problem looks something like this (although this example is relatively easy):

> Mallory reads x books per month. Over the course of y months, how many books does she read?
>
> (A) $x + y$ (B) $x - y$ (C) xy (D) $y - x$ (E) $\dfrac{x}{y}$

Notice that in this problem, the answer choices are not expressed in terms of numbers—they are expressed in terms of variables! This twist can make the problem much harder to think through. Luckily, there are several different techniques that we can apply to any VIC problem. These techniques will be the primary focus of this chapter.

As a simple solution process for this example, we can pretend that we were given numbers rather than variables. If, for example, Mallory reads 4 books per month for 5 months, she reads $4 \times 5 = 20$ books. Now, we switch back to variables. If she reads x books per month for y months, she will read $x \times y = xy$ books. Therefore (C) is the correct answer.

Some additional points to consider about VICs:

- **VIC problems are always Problem Solving problems.** The reason is simple: Data Sufficiency questions always have the SAME answer choices. Therefore we can only have variables in the answer choices for Problem Solving questions.
- **VIC problems always test some other math content.** For example, a VICs question may test you on percents, or on geometry, or on word problem translation or algebraic manipulation. Therefore, if we can categorize the VIC problem as some other type of problem as well, then we can often use the techniques suited for that type of problem to help solve the VIC problem. For instance, the example given above is a **Word Translations VIC** question involving Rates & Work.
- **VIC problems can generally be solved in more than one way.** In this chapter we will see multiple techniques for solving VIC problems, as well as advantages and drawbacks of each of these techniques.
- **Some VIC problems require you to invent variables to solve them algebraically.** Sometimes in a VIC problem, you may need to create intermediate unknowns that are not part of the final answer, but that help you to think through the problem. We will explore this issue in greater detail later in this chapter.
- **For some VIC problems, you cannot pick numbers for every variable in the problem.** Picking numbers, as we shall see, is a powerful technique to solve many VIC questions. However, in a VIC question with multiple variables, the value of one (or more) of the variables may depend upon the values you pick for the other variables. We will explore this issue in greater detail later in this chapter.

VIC problems can almost always be solved in more than one way.

VIC STRATEGY

Example VIC Problems

This section contains examples of the 4 most common types of VIC problems you will encounter on the GMAT:

- Word Translations VICs
- Algebra VICs
- Percent VICs
- Geometry VICs

VIC problems typically fall into one of 4 categories: word problems, algebra, percents, or geometry.

WORD TRANSLATIONS VIC EXAMPLE

Jack bought x pounds of candy at d dollars per pound. If he ate w pounds of his candy and sold the rest to Jill for m dollars per pound, how much money did Jack spend, in dollars, net of Jill's payment?

(A) $xd - wm$ (B) $xm - wd$ (C) $xd - xm + wm$

(D) $xd + xm - xw$ (E) $2xd - xm$

If all but one of the unknown quantities in this problem were replaced with numbers, this problem would be a standard Algebraic Translations problem. We would set up algebraic equations and solve for the remaining unknown.

Other Word Translations VIC problems involve specific types of word problems, such as Rates & Work or Ratios problems. For more on solving Word Translations problems, see the Manhattan GMAT *Word Translations* Strategy Guide.

ALGEBRA VIC EXAMPLE

If $\dfrac{abc}{72} = \dfrac{2}{d}$, which of the following expressions is equivalent to $ab - 2$?

(A) 72 (B) $\dfrac{72}{cd}$ (C) $\dfrac{144}{cd}$ (D) $\dfrac{144 - 2cd}{cd}$ (E) $\dfrac{144a - 2cd}{cd}$

Unlike Word Translations VIC problems, Algebra VIC problems have variables with no outside meaning: that is, the variables do not represent anything in the real world. One technique to solve this example problem is to use algebraic manipulation to isolate the expression "$ab - 2$" on one side of the equation. Whatever ends up on the other side of the equation should match one of the answer choices.

PERCENT VIC EXAMPLE

If x percent of y is equal to y percent less than z, what is y in terms of x and z?

(A) $\dfrac{100(x+z)}{x}$ (B) $\dfrac{100x}{x+z}$ (C) $\dfrac{100(x+z)}{x-z}$ (D) $\dfrac{100z}{x-z}$ (E) $\dfrac{100z}{x+z}$

In some respects, this type of VIC question is an extension of Word Translations VIC questions. We interpret the statement about the unknowns and try to devise an algebraic equation or equations matching the problem. The variables may or may not have outside meaning.

*Manhattan*GMAT*Prep
the new standard

An added wrinkle is working with percents. The term "*x* percent", for example, can be translated as $\dfrac{x}{100}$, and "*y* percent less than" can be translated as $1 - \dfrac{y}{100}$. Also, some Percent VIC questions will touch on topics specific to percent problems, such as percent change. For more on Percent problems, see the "Percents" chapter of the Manhattan GMAT *Fractions, Decimals & Percents* Strategy Guide.

GEOMETRY VIC EXAMPLE

A circular swimming pool is enclosed in a square fence, such that each side of the fence touches the circumference of the pool. What is the area of the swimming pool if the perimeter of the fence is *q* meters?

(A) $q^2\pi$ (B) $(q^2 - q)\pi$ (C) $\dfrac{q^2\pi}{4}$ (D) $\dfrac{q^2\pi}{16}$ (E) $\dfrac{q^2\pi}{64}$

This problem would be challenging enough if we were given numbers rather than variables: we would need to draw a diagram and use principles of Geometry to work through the problem step by step. The fact that variables are given instead of numbers makes the problem even more challenging. For more on solving Geometry problems, see the Manhattan GMAT *Geometry* Strategy Guide.

Three Strategies for Solving VICs

We can solve most VIC problems using any of three methods:

(1) Direct Algebra: Sometimes we can simply see the correct algebraic translation of the problem. For example, in the introductory problem involving Mallory, some people would be able to see right away that *xy* expresses the number of books she reads over the relevant time period. For Algebra VICs, this method generally involves manipulating the equations as needed until the solution is obtained. As the problems become more challenging, direct algebraic translation/manipulation may become too difficult or dangerous. However, this method can be very fast, because little or no intermediate work needs to be done.

(2) Pick Numbers and Calculate a Target: This method is especially useful when you cannot immediately see the proper algebraic translation or manipulation of the problem, and when it seems unlikely that wrestling with the algebra will yield success. Picking numbers and calculating a Target value can be applied to most VIC problems. The procedure involves the following steps:

  (1) Picking numbers for all or most of the unknowns in the problem
  (2) Using those numbers to calculate the answer to the problem—the "Target"
  (3) Plugging the numbers you have picked into each answer choice to see which answer choice yields the same value as your Target.

Note that this method has potential pitfalls. You may accidentally pick numbers that result in 2 or more answer choices yielding the Target value. Smart Numbers (discussed later) minimize but do not eliminate this possibility. Also, this method often requires a lot of computation, which can slow you down or lead you to make a fatal calculation error.

VIC problems can usually be solved in any of 3 different ways: direct algebraic translation/ manipulation, picking numbers and calculating a target value, or a hybrid of the two.

*Manhattan*GMAT*Prep
the new standard

(3)The Hybrid Method: This method adopts the best of both methods detailed above. You pick numbers to help you think through the problem. However, rather than plug these numbers into the answer choices, you use the numbers to think through the computations, and therefore the matching algebra, step by step. This method takes advantage of the use of concrete numbers, rather than variables, to think through the problem. Moreover, the method saves time, as we avoid plugging a bunch of values into the answer choices and computing each result.

VIC Strategies In Action: Example

Let us return to the Jack and Jill candy problem to see these strategies in action.

> Jack bought x pounds of candy at d dollars per pound. If he ate w pounds of his candy and sold the rest to Jill for m dollars per pound, how much money did Jack spend, in dollars, net of Jill's payment?
>
> (A) $xd - wm$ (B) $xm - wd$ (C) $xd - xm + wm$
> (D) $xd + xm - xw$ (E) $2xd - xm$

We will first solve this problem using the **Pick Numbers and Calculate a Target** methodology.

The **first step** is to pick numbers for each variable. It can be helpful to use a chart. There are several guidelines to keep in mind when picking numbers:

1. NEVER pick the numbers 1 or 0. (For Percent VICs, also avoid 100—it is too easy to confuse this 100 with the 100 needed to convert percents to decimals.)
2. Make sure all the numbers that you pick are DIFFERENT.
3. Pick SMALL numbers.
4. Try to pick PRIME numbers, to minimize the likelihood of ending up with redundant results when you plug your values into the answers.
5. Avoid picking numbers that appear as a coefficient in several answer choices.

Variable	Number	Description
x	11	pounds Jack bought
d	3	price per pound in store
w	7	pounds Jack ate
m	2	price Jill paid per pound

The table above shows the numbers that we chose for each variable, using these guidelines. Notice that the numbers are all different, prime and relatively small. You do not need to write descriptions for each, though doing so may help.

The **second step** is to answer the question, walking through the logic with the numbers that we have picked.

Jack bought 11 pounds of candy at $3 per pound. Therefore, he spent $33.
~~Jack ate 7 pounds of his candy and sold the rest to Jill. Therefore, he sold 4 pounds to Jill.~~
Jack sold the 4 pounds to Jill at $2 per pound. Therefore, Jill paid $8 for the candy.

How much money did Jack spend overall? He spent $33 on candy and sold $8 worth of that candy to Jill. Therefore, Jack spent $25, net of the payment he received from Jill.

*Manhattan*GMAT*Prep
the new standard

Once you have arrived at an answer, circle it on your scrap paper. This is your TARGET!

⟶ **TARGET**

The **third and final step** is to test each answer choice. Plug the numbers you have picked into each answer choice. Whichever answer choice yields your Target value is the correct solution to the problem:

Variable	Number	Description
x	11	pounds Jack bought
d	3	price per pound in store
w	7	pounds Jack ate
m	2	price Jill paid per pound

(A) $xd - wm = (11)(3) - (7)(2) = 33 - 14 = 19$ **Incorrect**
(B) $xm - wd = (11)(2) - (7)(3) = 22 - 21 = 1$ **Incorrect**
(C) $xd - xm + wm = (11)(3) - (11)(2) + (7)(2) = 33 - 22 + 14 = 25$ **CORRECT**
(D) $xd + xm - xw = (11)(3) + (11)(2) - (11)(7) = 33 + 22 - 77 = -22$ **Incorrect**
(E) $2xd - xm = (2)(11)(3) - (11)(2) = 66 - 22 = 44$ **Incorrect**

The correct answer is **(C)**, as this is the only choice which yields the Target value of 25.

When solving VICs, keep in mind that **you should ideally test _every_ answer choice, even if you have already found one that equals your Target value.**

Why? Sometimes you will find that more than one answer choice yields your Target value. In such cases, you should pick new numbers and test these remaining answer choices again, until only one answer choice yields your Target value. By picking smart numbers we can minimize the likelihood of getting multiple answer choices with the same result, but this outcome still may happen occasionally.

Notice that we could have stopped calculating part-way through on answer choices (B) and (E), because at some point we may realize that the result cannot possibly equal our Target of 25. In both cases, the number will be much smaller than 25. Once you realize that an answer choice CANNOT equal the Target value, **stop calculating that answer choice!**

Next, we will solve this problem using the **Direct Algebra** method. The best thing to do in this situation is to break the problem down into manageable parts. Then think through the algebra step by step, writing down expressions for intermediate quantities:

STEP	STATEMENT FROM PROBLEM	THOUGHT PROCESS
1	"Jack bought x pounds of candy at d dollars per pound..."	"Jack spent xd dollars originally..."
2	"...he ate w pounds of his candy and sold the rest to Jill..."	"...he now has $(x - w)$ pounds of candy remaining..."
3	"...sold the rest to Jill for m dollars per pound..."	"...he sold the $(x - w)$ pounds of candy to Jill for m dollars a pound, so $(x - w)m$ dollars is revenue..."

When you use the strategy of picking numbers to find a target value, you should ideally test EVERY answer choice.

You can now use this thought process to write the algebraic expression for the problem: he spent *xd* dollars on the candy, but he recouped some of that amount from Jill:

$$xd - (x - w)m$$

We can distribute this expression to see that it matches answer choice (**C**) perfectly:

$$xd - xm + wm$$

Finally, we will solve this problem using the **Hybrid Method**. Recall that the goal of this method is to pick numbers to help you think through the problem, using the numbers to guide you through the computations, and therefore the algebra, step by step. Once again, the best thing to do is to break the problem down into manageable parts. We will use the same numbers that we used in the **Pick Numbers and Calculate a Target** strategy:

Variable	Number	Description
x	11	pounds Jack bought
d	3	price per pound in store
w	7	pounds Jack ate
m	2	price Jill paid per pound

STEP	STATEMENT FROM PROBLEM	THOUGHT PROCESS
1	"Jack bought *x* pounds of candy at *d* dollars per pound..."	"Jack spent 11 × 3 = 33 dollars originally, which is *x* × *d*, or *xd* dollars..."
2	"...he ate *w* pounds of his candy and sold the rest to Jill..."	"...he now has 11 − 7 = 4 pounds of candy, which is (*x* − *w*) pounds..."
3	"...sold the rest to Jill for *m* dollars per pound..."	"...he sold the 4 pounds of candy to Jill for 2 dollars a pound and got 8 dollars... let's see, that's (*x* − *w*) × *m* dollars..."

We are now in the same position we were in after thinking step-by-step through the "Direct Algebraic Translations" strategy. We know the components that we need to answer the question, and we simply need to put them together:

$$xd - (x - w) \times m$$
$$xd - (x - w)m$$
$$xd - xm + wm$$

Once again, the correct answer is (**C**). The advantage of using numbers in this Hybrid Method is that you make the algebra concrete, so you are less likely to go astray. At the same time, you retain the speed of the Direct Algebra method. You have to become comfortable shifting back and forth between arithmetic and algebra, however. In a sense, you are performing two processes at once, using one to guide the other. This "back and forth" sounds harder than it is, and it can actually improve your algebraic confidence, but you must practice the technique.

Pros and Cons of Different VIC Strategies

Below is a list of pros and cons associated with each VIC solution technique that we have discussed. Be sure to consider all of these pros and cons, and practice each technique!

(1) Direct Algebraic Translation/Manipulation

PROS	CONS
1. Generally very fast	1. Difficult to double-check answer
2. Goes hand-in-hand with needed algebraic translation skills	2. Susceptible to built-in algebraic or logical traps in the problem
3. Minimal computation, reducing arithmetic errors	3. Translating/manipulating the algebra may be difficult to do on some VIC problems
4. Most effective on problems with many unknowns	

(2) Pick Numbers and Calculate Target

PROS	CONS
1. General method that can be used to solve nearly all VIC problems	1. Often time-intensive
2. Arithmetic is sometimes much easier than algebra, especially on advanced VIC problems	2. Prone to arithmetic errors
3. Effective at some problems where algebraic translation or manipulation is particularly tricky	3. For some problems, some variables are dependent on others, so you cannot pick a value for each
4. Most effective on problems with few unknowns (1 or 2)	4. Problems with many unknowns can be very time-consuming
	5. Sometimes you must use the method more than once to find values that yield a unique solution

(3) Hybrid Method

PROS	CONS
1. Uses numbers rather than variables to think through algebra	1. Difficult to double-check answer
2. Can be broken down into component steps	2. Susceptible to built-in algebraic or logical traps in the problem
3. Often very fast	3. Requires shifting back and forth between arithmetic and algebra
4. Minimal computation, reducing math errors	4. Some advanced VIC problems are difficult to solve this way

Each of the VIC solutions strategies has its pros and cons—practice each to develop a sense of when to use which technique!

More VIC Examples

Let us revisit the example problems that we have not yet solved.

<u>ALGEBRA VIC EXAMPLE</u>

If $\dfrac{abc}{72} = \dfrac{2}{d}$, which of the following expressions is equivalent to $ab - 2$?

(A) 72   (B) $\dfrac{72}{cd}$ (C) $\dfrac{144}{cd}$ (D) $\dfrac{144-2cd}{cd}$ (E) $\dfrac{144a-2cd}{cd}$

> You can use unconventional algebraic manipulations to solve for the expression you are being asked about in Algebra VIC problems—just be careful not to make an algebraic mistake!

As we saw earlier, one technique to solve the problem is to use algebraic manipulation to isolate the expression "$ab - 2$" on one side of the equation. Whatever ends up on the right-hand side of the equation should match one of the answer choices. This is the **Direct Algebra** approach. The first step is to solve for ab:

$$\frac{abc}{72} = \frac{2}{d} \qquad\qquad abcd = 144 \qquad\qquad ab = \frac{144}{cd}$$

Next, we have to subtract two from both sides of the equation. This step is difficult for many people to see, because we are trained from an early age to use algebraic manipulations to make algebraic equations and expressions simpler, not more complicated. However on the GMAT, occasionally we have to use algebra to make things **more complicated** to answer the specific question we are being asked.

Also notice that none of the answer choices has two terms. Therefore after we subtract 2 from both sides of the equation, we should combine the right-hand side of the equation into one term:

$$ab - 2 = \frac{144}{cd} - 2 \qquad\qquad ab - 2 = \frac{144}{cd} - \frac{2cd}{cd} \qquad\qquad ab - 2 = \frac{144 - 2cd}{cd}$$

Thus the correct answer is **(D)**. Notice that it would have been very easy to make an algebraic mistake along the way, and end up with a different answer. We might have ended up with the expression in answer choice (E), for example. The primary problem with using the Direct Algebra approach is that if you make a mistake along the way, you may not catch it!

In fact, the GMAT can predict what other values you may end up with, because algebra mistakes are not random. Understanding the likely errors, the GMAT presents the results of erroneous algebra as tempting answer choices. So, if you are going to use Direct Algebra to solve a problem, you must be confident that you are doing the algebra correctly.

*Manhattan*GMAT Prep
the new standard

Let us now solve the problem using the **Pick Numbers and Calculate a Target** approach. Notice that because the variables are related to each other through an equation, we CANNOT pick a value for each variable. We must pick a value for all but one of the variables and then solve for the value of the remaining variable. Let us say that we decide that $a = 2$, $b = 3$, and $c = 4$. Plugging these into the equation determines d.

Variable	Value
a	2
b	3
c	4
d	6

Solved for BEFORE calculating Target value!

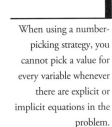

$$\frac{abc}{72} = \frac{2}{d} \rightarrow \frac{(2)(3)(4)}{72} = \frac{2}{d} \rightarrow \frac{24}{72} = \frac{2}{d} \rightarrow \frac{1}{3} = \frac{2}{d} \rightarrow d = 6$$

Next, we find the Target value by plugging the numbers we have selected into the expression $ab - 2$: $(2)(3) - 2 = 6 - 2 = $ **4**. Note that the value of d, which we solved for, is NOT the Target value!

When using a number-picking strategy, you cannot pick a value for every variable whenever there are explicit or implicit equations in the problem.

Use the Target to test each answer choice. We plug in 2 for a, 3 for b, 4 for c, and 6 for d, in search of our Target value of 4:

(A) 72   **Incorrect**

(B) $\dfrac{72}{cd} = \dfrac{72}{(4)(6)} = \dfrac{72}{24} = 3$ **Incorrect**

(C) $\dfrac{144}{cd} = \dfrac{144}{(4)(6)} = \dfrac{144}{24} = 6$ **Incorrect**

(D) $\dfrac{144 - 2cd}{cd} = \dfrac{144 - (2)(4)(6)}{(4)(6)} = \dfrac{96}{24} = 4$ **CORRECT**

(E) $\dfrac{144a - 2cd}{cd} = \dfrac{(144)(2) - (2)(4)(6)}{(4)(6)} = \dfrac{240}{24} = 10$ **Incorrect**

When you use this method, be sure to test every answer choice to make sure that only one produces the Target value.

Also, notice how similar many of the calculations are across the answer choices. If you notice such similarities, you can **re-use chunks of calculations from one answer choice to other answers choices** that contain the same expressions. This will save you valuable time.

<u>PERCENT VIC EXAMPLE</u>

If x percent of y is equal to y percent less than z, what is y in terms of x and z?

(A) $\dfrac{100(x + z)}{x}$ (B) $\dfrac{100x}{x + z}$ (C) $\dfrac{100(x + z)}{x - z}$ (D) $\dfrac{100z}{x - z}$ (E) $\dfrac{100z}{x + z}$

Because this problem is given in story format, we can think about it a little like a Word Translations VIC question. We also have to consider how to deal with percents. The term "x percent," as given in this problem, does NOT mean x.

For example, if $x = 30$, then x percent means 30 percent, or $\dfrac{30}{100} = 0.3$, NOT 30.

Therefore, you can think of "percent" in this problem as "divided by 100." Also, "of" in this type of problem often translates to "times." Thus, "x percent of y" translates to "x percent TIMES y," which is $\left(\dfrac{x}{100}\right)y = \dfrac{xy}{100}$. Finally, in this problem we have "y percent less than z." This is equivalent to a percent change in z, meaning "z, minus y percent of z":

$$z - \frac{y}{100} \text{ of } z = z - \left(\frac{y}{100}\right)z = z\left(1 - \frac{y}{100}\right)$$

Practice the translations for common Percent VIC statements, such as "x percent of y" and "z percent more than w."

Similarly, we would have translated "y percent more than z" as "z, plus y percent of z":

$$z + \frac{y}{100} \text{ of } z = z + \left(\frac{y}{100}\right)z = z\left(1 + \frac{y}{100}\right)$$

Because we are told that x percent of y must equal y percent less than z, we can set the two expressions equal to each other, then solve for y:

$$\left(\frac{x}{100}\right)y = z\left(1 - \frac{y}{100}\right) \qquad\qquad \frac{y}{100}(x + z) = z$$

$$\frac{xy}{100} = z - \frac{zy}{100} \qquad\qquad \frac{y}{100} = \frac{z}{x + z}$$

$$\frac{xy}{100} + \frac{zy}{100} = z \qquad\qquad y = \frac{100z}{x + z}$$

Therefore the correct answer is (E), which we reached using the **Direct Algebra** method.

If we had trouble setting up or carrying out the algebra for this problem, we could have used the **Hybrid Method**: that is, pick numbers for the variables and use those numbers to guide our algebraic setup through the problem. As was true in the previous problem, the variables are linked by an equation. Thus, we must pick numbers for only two of the variables, then solve for the other variable. Let us pick 30 for x and 40 for y:

STEP	STATEMENT	THOUGHT PROCESS
1	"x percent of y..."	"30 percent of 40 is 12, so we need $(0.3) \times 40$... OK, that is $\left(\dfrac{30}{100}\right)40$, so the expression must be $\left(\dfrac{x}{100}\right)y$ "
2	"...equals y percent less than z..."	"...OK, so 12 equals 40% less than what number? $12 = z - 40\%$ of z... that means $12 = 0.6z$, so z is 20! Now I know the right-hand side of the equation looks like $z - 0.4z$, which is $z - \dfrac{40}{100}z$ or $z - \left(\dfrac{y}{100}\right)z$ ..."

Now we have both sides of the equation correctly expressed in terms of x, y and z, and we can solve the problem algebraically just as we did in the **Direct Algebra** approach.

Finally, you could use the **Pick Numbers and Calculate a Target** method: pick numbers for x and y (solving for z) and then plug your x and z values into the answer choices to see which one gives you the correct value for y. (Alternatively, you could pick values for x and z and solve for y.) This method is useful when you cannot see the proper algebraic translation of the problem, and it seems unlikely that intermediate work will help, or if you are having problems manipulating the equation to solve for y.

Once again, let's select 30 for x and 40 for y, and solve for z:

30 percent of 40 is equal to 40 percent less than z...

30% of 40 = 40% less than z...

$(0.3)40 = z - (0.4)z$

$12 = 0.6z \qquad z = 20$

Variable	Value
x	30
y	40
z	(20)

Solved for BEFORE calculating Target value!

For Percent VIC problems you should avoid picking 100, but you usually should pick multiples of 10 that are easy to work with, such as 20, 30, 40, or 50.

We picked 40 for y, so 40 is our Target value:

(A) $\dfrac{100(x+z)}{x} = \dfrac{100(30+20)}{30} = \dfrac{5{,}000}{30} = \dfrac{500}{3}$ **Incorrect**

(B) $\dfrac{100x}{x+z} = \dfrac{100(30)}{30+20} = \dfrac{3{,}000}{50} = 60$ **Incorrect**

(C) $\dfrac{100(x+z)}{x-z} = \dfrac{100(30+20)}{30-20} = \dfrac{5{,}000}{10} = 50$ **Incorrect**

(D) $\dfrac{100z}{x-z} = \dfrac{100(20)}{30-20} = \dfrac{2{,}000}{10} = 200$ **Incorrect**

(E) $\dfrac{100z}{x+z} = \dfrac{100(20)}{(30+20)} = \dfrac{2{,}000}{50} = 40$ **CORRECT**

GEOMETRY VIC EXAMPLE

A circular swimming pool is enclosed in a square fence, such that each side of the fence touches the circumference of the pool. What is the area of the swimming pool if the perimeter of the fence is q meters?

(A) $q^2\pi$ (B) $(q^2 - q)\pi$ (C) $\dfrac{q^2\pi}{4}$ (D) $\dfrac{q^2\pi}{16}$ (E) $\dfrac{q^2\pi}{64}$

One of the principles discussed in the Manhattan GMAT *Geometry* Strategy Guide is that for any Geometry problem, we need to draw a diagram based on the description given in the problem and use principles of Geometry to work through the problem step by step. The fact that variables are given instead of numbers makes the problem more challenging.

First, let us draw a diagram of this problem and work through the problem using the **Direct Algebra** approach.

*Manhattan*GMAT*Prep
the new standard

Notice that we have INVENTED a variable, r, to represent the radius of the circle. We do not need to do this—the problem can be solved without adding this variable. Moreover, we will need to eliminate r from our solution before we are finished, because r is not part of the answer choices. However, breaking the problem down further by creating intermediate variables can sometimes make the solution process easier.

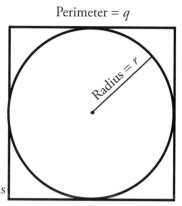

Perimeter = q

From the Manhattan GMAT *Geometry* Strategy Guide, we know that the area of the circle is equal to πr^2. We now simply need to solve for r in terms of q and plug this solution into the expression πr^2 to solve the problem.

ALWAYS draw a diagram for a Geometry VIC problem, whether you are picking numbers or not!

Notice that if the perimeter of a square is q, then the 4 sides, which must all be equal in length to each other, must be $\dfrac{q}{4}$. Therefore, each side of the square is equal to $\dfrac{q}{4}$. Notice also that the diameter of the circle is equal to the length of the side of the square: if we draw a diameter through the middle of the circle, it is equal in length to the topmost or bottommost side of the square.

Since the diameter of the square is equal to twice the radius, we have:

$$\text{Side of square} = \text{diameter of circle} = 2r = \frac{q}{4}$$

$$r = \frac{q}{8}$$

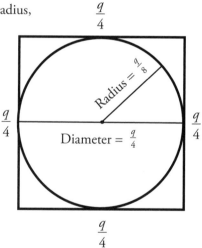

Thus, the area of the swimming pool is

$\pi r^2 = \pi \left(\dfrac{q}{8}\right)^2 = \dfrac{\pi q^2}{64}$. The correct answer is **(E)**.

Alternatively, we could use the **Pick Numbers and Calculate a Target** strategy. Let us say that $q = 24$. Then each side of the external square equals 6, so the diameter of the circle equals 6, and the radius of the circle equals 3. (Notice that we picked a relatively big value for q, one that is divisible by 4 and then by 2, so that we can find an integer value for the radius.) Therefore, the area of the circle, πr^2, equals 9π. 9π becomes our Target value.

(A) $q^2\pi = (24)^2\pi = 576\pi$ **Incorrect**

(B) $(q^2 - q)\pi = (24^2 - 24)\pi = 552\pi$ **Incorrect**

(C) $\dfrac{q^2\pi}{4} = \dfrac{(24)^2\pi}{4} = (12)^2\pi = 144\pi$ **Incorrect**

(D) $\dfrac{q^2\pi}{16} = \dfrac{(24)^2\pi}{16} = (6)^2\pi = 36\pi$ **Incorrect**

(E) $\dfrac{q^2\pi}{64} = \dfrac{(24)^2\pi}{64} = (3)^2\pi = 9\pi$ **CORRECT**

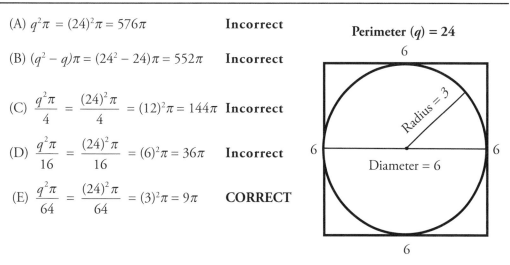

Perimeter (q) = 24
6
6   6
Radius = 3
Diameter = 6
6

Do not be afraid to create intermediate variables to represent key unknowns when solving a VIC problem. Just remember that your solution cannot contain these intermediate variables.

Which VIC Strategy Should You Choose?

We have seen several different approaches to solving VIC problems. Each technique has its strengths and drawbacks. Preferably, you will become comfortable using any of the approaches outlined in this chapter. However, some people may find that they are much more comfortable with one approach over the others. Here are a few basic guidelines to help you determine which approach you should use as your main line of attack:

(1) Ideally, you will become comfortable with all three approaches laid out in this chapter. Some problems are much easier to solve using one technique over another. That said, many people will end up preferring one technique over the others for most VIC problems.

(2) Be sure to practice each technique. You may find that by practicing a particular technique, you become faster or more accurate when using it. In particular, the **Direct Algebra** and **Hybrid Method** approaches to VIC problems tend to be much faster than the **Pick Numbers and Calculate a Target** approach. The reason is that, if you are successful, you will avoid wasting time performing calculations on the four incorrect answer choices.

(3) When in doubt, you can almost always use the Pick Number and Calculate a Target approach. This technique is often preferred by people who are not as comfortable with algebra. It is generally most effective when there are only a few variables in the problem. If the problem has many variables, the Picking Numbers method can require lengthy and detailed calculations that you must get precisely right.

That said, if you are trying to figure out the algebraic manipulation but you get stuck, **you should immediately switch to a number-picking strategy!** Some very difficult VIC problems in *The Official Guide* are easily solved with test numbers. These problems are considered difficult because most people try algebra but then never switch strategies. Never give up on a VIC problem before picking numbers.

VIC STRATEGY

Very occasionally, a VIC problem can only be solved by direct algebra, because the variables are <u>already</u> defined as numbers. These numbers are chosen to be huge or otherwise unwieldy, as in the following example:

> If $x = 5^{20}$ and $y = 5^{19}$, what is $x - y$, in terms of y?
>
> (A) $-5y$ (B) y (C) $4y$ (D) $5y$ (E) $19y$

Here, we <u>must</u> connect the given values of x and y in some way. Since $5^{20} = 5 \cdot 5^{19}$, we can write $x = 5y$. Now the target expression $x - y$ can be rewritten as $5y - y = 4y$. The correct answer is (C).

If the variables in a VIC problem are already defined as numbers, find the equation that relates the numbers. This will be the same equation that relates the variables.

Problem Set

Solve each problem with a tracking chart.

1. If x, y, and z are consecutive integers, which of the following must be an integer?

   (A) $\dfrac{x + 2y + 2z}{3}$ (B) $\dfrac{x + y + z}{3}$ (C) $\dfrac{x + y + z}{2}$ (D) $\dfrac{x + y + z}{6}$

2. Maria will be x years old in 12 years. How old was she 9 years ago?

   (A) $x - 3$ (B) $x - 20$ (C) $x + 3$ (D) $x - 21$ (E) $x + 6$

3. If Cecil reads T pages per minute, how many hours will it take him to read 500 pages?

   (A) $\dfrac{500}{T}$ (B) $\dfrac{500}{60T}$ (C) $\dfrac{5T}{6}$ (D) $3000T$ (E) $\dfrac{60T}{500}$

4. A town's oldest inhabitant is x years older than the sum of the ages of the Lee triplets. If the oldest inhabitant is now J years old, how old will one of the triplets be in 20 years?

   (A) $\dfrac{J - 50}{3}$ (B) $\dfrac{3(J + 20)}{x}$ (C) $\dfrac{J + x - 50}{3}$ (D) $\dfrac{J - x + 60}{3}$ (E) $\dfrac{J + x - 20}{3}$

5. K is an even number, and G is an integer. Which of the following cannot be odd?

   (A) $K + G$ (B) KG (C) $K - G$ (D) $2K + G$ (E) $3(K + G)$

6. Mr. and Mrs. Wiley have a child every J years. Their oldest child is now T years old. If they have a child 2 years from now, how many children will they have in total?

   (A) $\dfrac{T + 2}{J} + 1$ (B) $JT + 1$ (C) $\dfrac{J}{T} + \dfrac{1}{T}$ (D) $TJ - 1$ (E) $\dfrac{J + T}{J}$

7. If $\dfrac{N}{T} = \dfrac{P}{M}$, then MT is equal to which of the following?

   (A) NP (B) $\dfrac{NP}{T}$ (C) $\dfrac{MN^2}{P}$ (D) $\dfrac{NP}{M}$ (E) $\dfrac{PT^2}{N}$

8. The average of A, B, and C is D. What is the average of A and B?

   (A) $\dfrac{A + B - C}{3}$ (B) $\dfrac{3D - C}{2}$ (C) $\dfrac{3D - A - B + C}{3}$ (D) $\dfrac{3D + A + B + C}{4}$ (E) 9

9. If Cassandra wins M dollars in a billiards tournament and J dollars at each of seven county fairs, what is her average prize (in dollars)?

   (A) $\dfrac{M + 7J}{8}$ (B) $\dfrac{M + J}{7}$ (C) $\dfrac{M + 7J}{7}$ (D) $\dfrac{7M + J}{8}$ (E) $M + \dfrac{J}{7}$

10. If $\dfrac{x^2 - 11x + 28}{L} = 9$, which of the following is equivalent to L?

    (A) $L(x^2 - 11x + 19)$ (B) $\dfrac{9}{x^2 + 11x - 28}$ (C) $\dfrac{(x - 7)(x - 4)}{9}$

(D) $\dfrac{(x-7)(x-4)}{9x^2+28}$ (E) $\dfrac{x^2-11x+37}{9}$

11. If $m-\dfrac{n}{m}=\dfrac{5-m^2}{m}$, which of the following is equal to n?

(A) -5 (B) $2m^2-5$ (C) m^2-5 (D) $5-m^2$ (E) $5-2m^2$

12. a, b, c and d are positive numbers. If $ab=c$ and $\dfrac{a}{b}=d$, what is $a+b$?

(A) $d\sqrt{cd}$ (B) $\dfrac{\sqrt{cd}}{d}$ (C) $\dfrac{\sqrt{cd}+d}{d}$ (D) $\dfrac{d(\sqrt{cd}+1)}{d}$ (E) $\dfrac{\sqrt{cd}\,(d+1)}{d}$

13. Kate can run A feet in B seconds. Amelia can run C feet in D seconds. In a race of 1,000 feet, by how many seconds will Kate beat Amelia (assuming they both run at these rates)?

(A) $\dfrac{1{,}000(AD-BC)}{AC}$ (B) $\dfrac{1{,}000BC-1{,}000DA}{AC}$ (C) $\dfrac{AB-CD}{1{,}000}$ (D) $\dfrac{AD-CB}{1{,}000}$

14. x is what percent of y, in terms of x and y?

(A) $100xy$ (B) $\dfrac{100x}{y}$ (C) $\dfrac{100y}{x}$ (D) $\dfrac{x}{100y}$ (E) $\dfrac{y}{100x}$

15. A furniture salesman sells chairs, sofas, and tables. One day, $\dfrac{1}{4}$ of the items sold were sofas and $\dfrac{2}{5}$ of the remaining items sold were chairs. If T tables were sold, how many sofas were sold in terms of T?

(A) $\dfrac{9}{5}T$ (B) $\dfrac{3}{2}T$ (C) $\dfrac{2}{3}T$ (D) $\dfrac{5}{8}T$ (E) $\dfrac{5}{9}T$

Note: Most answer explanations in this section demonstrate only one VIC solution technique. However, most of the problems can be solved using any of the three VIC solution techniques described in this chapter.

1. **(B):** Using the **Pick Numbers and Calculate a Target** strategy, we assign values to each variable, and record them in a table. Then, we test each answer choice.

variable	number
x	2
y	3
z	4

Note that we must pick *consecutive* integers, as specified in the question.

(A) $\dfrac{x + 2y + 2z}{3} = \dfrac{2 + 2(3) + 2(4)}{3} = \dfrac{16}{3}$

(B) $\dfrac{x + y + z}{3} = \dfrac{2 + 3 + 4}{3} = \dfrac{9}{3} = 3$

(C) $\dfrac{x + y + z}{2} = \dfrac{2 + 3 + 4}{2} = \dfrac{9}{2}$

(D) $\dfrac{x + y + z}{6} = \dfrac{2 + 3 + 4}{6} = \dfrac{9}{6} = \dfrac{3}{2}$

The only answer choice that yields an integer is (B).

2. **(D):** Using the **Pick Numbers and Calculate a Target** strategy, we pick $x = 50$. If Maria will be 50 years old in 12 years, she is currently 38 years old. Therefore, she was 29 years old 9 years ago. Test each answer choice to find the one that yields the target value of 29.

(A) $x - 3 = 50 - 3 = 47$ Incorrect
(B) $x - 20 = 50 - 20 = 30$ Incorrect
(C) $x + 3 = 50 + 3 = 53$ Incorrect
(D) $x - 21 = 50 - 21 = 29$ CORRECT
(E) $x + 6 = 50 + 6 = 56$ Incorrect

3. **(B):** Using the **Pick Numbers and Calculate a Target** strategy, we choose $T = 10$. If Cecil reads 10 pages per minute, he will read a 500-page novel in 50 minutes. This is equivalent to $\dfrac{50}{60}$, or $\dfrac{5}{6}$ hours. Test each

answer choice to find the one that yields the target value of $\dfrac{5}{6}$.

(A) $\dfrac{500}{T} = \dfrac{500}{10} = 50$ Incorrect

(B) $\dfrac{500}{60T} = \dfrac{500}{(60)(10)} = \dfrac{5}{6}$ CORRECT

(C) $\dfrac{5T}{6} = \dfrac{5(10)}{6} = \dfrac{50}{6}$ Incorrect

(D) $3000T = 3000(10) = 30{,}000$ Incorrect

(E) $\dfrac{60T}{500} = \dfrac{60(10)}{500} = \dfrac{6}{5}$ Incorrect

4. **(D):** Let us use the **Pick Numbers and Calculate a Target** strategy. If the oldest inhabitant is 100 years old, and he is 10 years older than the sum of the ages of the Lee triplets, each triplet is 30 years old. In 20 years, each triplet will be 50 years old. Test each answer choice to find the one that yields the Target value of 50.

variable	number
x	10
J	100

(A) $\dfrac{J-50}{3} = \dfrac{100-50}{3} = \dfrac{50}{3}$ Incorrect

(B) $\dfrac{3(J+20)}{x} = \dfrac{3(100+20)}{10} = 36$ Incorrect

(C) $\dfrac{J+x-50}{3} = \dfrac{100+10-50}{3} = \dfrac{60}{3} = 20$ Incorrect

(D) $\dfrac{J-x+60}{3} = \dfrac{100-10+60}{3} = 50$ CORRECT

(E) $\dfrac{J+x-20}{3} = \dfrac{100+10-20}{3} = 30$ Incorrect

5. **(B):** Using the **Pick Numbers and Calculate a Target** strategy, select an even number for K and an integer for G. Then, test each answer choice to find the one that does *not* yield an odd number.

variable	number
K	4
G	3

(A) $K + G = 4 + 3 = 7$ Incorrect
(B) $KG = 4 \times 3 = 12$ CORRECT
(C) $K - G = 4 - 3 = 1$ Incorrect
(D) $2K + G = 2(4) + 3 = 11$ Incorrect
(E) $3(K + G) = 3(4 + 3) = 21$ Incorrect

6. **(A):** If the Wileys have a child every 2 years and the oldest child is 12, they have 7 children, ages 0 (just born), 2, 4, 6, 8, 10, and 12. If they have another child 2 years from now, they will have 8 children. Test each answer choice to find the one that yields the Target value of 8.

variable	number
J	2
T	12

(A) $\dfrac{T+2}{J} + 1 = \dfrac{12+2}{2} + 1 = 8$ CORRECT

(B) $JT + 1 = 24 + 1 = 25$ Incorrect

(C) $\dfrac{J}{T} + \dfrac{1}{T} = \dfrac{2}{12} + \dfrac{1}{12} = \dfrac{1}{4}$ Incorrect

(D) $TJ - 1 = 24 - 1 = 23$ Incorrect

(E) $\dfrac{J+T}{J} = \dfrac{2+12}{2} = 7$ Incorrect

7. **(E)**: Let us use the **Pick Numbers and Calculate a Target** strategy. Select variables that will satisfy the equation $\dfrac{N}{T} = \dfrac{P}{M}$. If we select the values shown in the chart to the right, $MT = 3 \times 2 = 6$. Then, we test each answer choice to find the ones that yield the target number 6.

variable	number
N	6
T	2
P	9
M	3

(A) $NP = 6 \times 9 = 54$ Incorrect

(B) $\dfrac{NP}{T} = \dfrac{6 \times 9}{2} = 27$ Incorrect

(C) $\dfrac{MN^2}{P} = \dfrac{3 \times 6^2}{9} = 12$ Incorrect

(D) $\dfrac{NP}{M} = \dfrac{6 \times 9}{3} = 18$ Incorrect

(E) $\dfrac{PT^2}{N} = \dfrac{9 \times 2^2}{6} = 6$ CORRECT

You can also solve this by **Direct Algebra**: $\dfrac{N}{T} = \dfrac{P}{M}$ $NM = PT$ $M = \dfrac{PT}{N}$ $MT = \dfrac{PT^2}{N}$

8. **(B)**: If the average of A, B, and C is D, then $\dfrac{A+B+C}{3} = D$. Using the **Direct Algebra** strategy, we need to solve for the average of A and B, which is given by $\dfrac{A+B}{2}$, then see which answer choice matches our result:

$$\dfrac{A+B+C}{3} = D$$
$$A+B+C = 3D$$

$$A+B = 3D - C$$
$$\dfrac{A+B}{2} = \dfrac{3D-C}{2}$$

9. **(A)**: Using the **Hybrid Method**, we might decide that Cassandra wins 10 dollars in a billiards tournament (this is M) and 20 dollars at each of seven county fairs (this is J). In that case, her total prize money is $(10) + 7(20)$, which is $(M) + 7(J)$. Since she is in a total of 8 contests, her average is given by $\dfrac{M + 7J}{8}$. Thus the correct answer choice is (A).

10. **(C)**: Using the **Direct Algebra** approach, we can solve for L as follows:

$$9 = \dfrac{x^2 - 11x + 28}{L}$$
$$9L = x^2 - 11x + 28$$
$$L = \dfrac{x^2 - 11x + 28}{9}$$

Now we can factor the numerator and we have:

$$L = \frac{(x-7)(x-4)}{9}$$

11. **(B):** This Algebra VIC problem can be solved using the **Direct Algebra** method. However, note that it is very easy to make a mistake, because in the algebraic manipulation you may encounter a "double negative" that needs to be made positive:

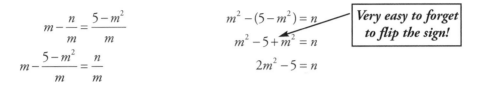

If you are not confident that you would spot this trap, then you might prefer to pick numbers.

12. **(E):** This difficult Algebra VIC problem can be solved using the **Direct Algebra** method, as demonstrated here. It should be noted, however, that the **Pick Numbers and Calculate a Target** method can be used by anyone who is unsure of how to do the algebra, and may in fact be easier to complete if smart numbers are chosen:

$$ab = c$$

$$\frac{a}{b} = d$$

$$a = db$$

$$(db)b = c$$

$$db^2 = c$$

$$b^2 = \frac{c}{d}$$

$$b = \sqrt{\frac{c}{d}}$$

$$a\left(\sqrt{\frac{c}{d}}\right) = c$$

$$a = \frac{c}{\sqrt{\frac{c}{d}}}$$

$$a = \frac{c}{\frac{\sqrt{cd}}{d}}$$

$$a = \frac{cd}{\sqrt{cd}}$$

$$a = \sqrt{cd}$$

$$a + b = \sqrt{cd} + \sqrt{\frac{c}{d}} = \sqrt{cd} + \frac{\sqrt{cd}}{d}$$

$$a + b = \frac{d\sqrt{cd} + \sqrt{cd}}{d} = \frac{\sqrt{cd}\,(d+1)}{d}$$

13. **(A):** This is a Rates & Work problem that can be solved using RTD Charts. We will use the **Hybrid Method** to think through the problem. Let us assume Kate can run 12 feet in 2 seconds, and Amelia can run 15 feet in 3 seconds. This means that $A = 12$, $B = 2$, $C = 15$, and $D = 3$. In that case, Kate is running at $12 \div 2 = 6$ feet per second and Amelia is running at $15 \div 3 = 5$ feet per second. (Notice that in the problem, Kate beats Amelia to the finish line, so we picked numbers that would make Kate faster.) We do not know the amount of time the two sprinters will be running, so we invent variables to represent their times. (We will later get rid of these new variables.) Now we can populate RTD charts for each sprinter:

the new standard

(units)	Rate (feet/sec)	×	Time (seconds)	=	Distance (feet)
Kate	$6 = \dfrac{A}{B}$	×	t_1	=	1,000

(units)	Rate (feet/sec)	×	Time (seconds)	=	Distance (feet)
Amelia	$5 = \dfrac{C}{D}$	×	t_2	=	1,000

Since Rate × Time = Distance, we can write equations to express the times for each sprinter:

$$\left(\frac{A}{B}\right)t_1 = 1,000 \qquad\qquad \left(\frac{C}{D}\right)t_2 = 1,000$$

$$t_1 = \frac{1,000}{\dfrac{A}{B}} \qquad\qquad t_2 = \frac{1,000}{\dfrac{C}{D}}$$

$$t_1 = \frac{1,000\,B}{A} \qquad\qquad t_2 = \frac{1,000\,D}{C}$$

The problem asks for the difference in times. Since Kate will take less time to complete the race, we should

evaluate $t_2 - t_1$: $t_2 - t_1 = \dfrac{1,000\,D}{C} - \dfrac{1,000\,B}{A} = \dfrac{1,000(AD - BC)}{AC}$. Therefore **(A)** is the correct answer.

For more on solving Rates & Work problems, see the "Rates & Work" chapter of the Manhattan GMAT *Word Translations* Strategy Guide.

14. **(B):** This problem can be solved by using the **Direct Algebra** approach. "*x* is what percent of *y*" can be solved by creating an intermediate variable, such as *w*, to represent the percent of *y* that *x* equals, and then solve for that variable:

$$x = \frac{w}{100} \times y \qquad\qquad x = \frac{wy}{100} \qquad\qquad \frac{100x}{y} = w$$

Alternatively, you could use the **Hybrid Method**. Say *x* = 20 and *y* = 80. Then *x* is 25 percent of *y*. How

do we use 20 and 80 to arrive at 25? Simply divide *x* by *y*, then multiply by 100: $\dfrac{100x}{y}$.

15. **(E):** For this problem, you should use the **Hybrid Method**. Also, the problem is easier to think through if two intermediate variables are added: *S* for sofas sold, and *x* for total furniture items sold.

Assuming we choose 20 to equal *x*, then $\dfrac{1}{4}(20) = 5$ sofas were sold. This tells us that $S = \dfrac{1}{4}x$. Thus the remaining items total $20 - 5 = 15$ items. Algebraically, this is $x - \frac{1}{4}x = \frac{3}{4}x$. $\frac{2}{5}$ of these items are chairs,

so $\frac{2}{5}(15) = 6$ chairs are sold. Algebraically, this is $\frac{2}{5} \cdot \frac{3}{4}x = \frac{3}{10}x$ chairs. Therefore, $T =$

$15 - \left(\frac{2}{5}\right)\left(\frac{3}{4}\right)20 = 9$. Algebraically, this is $T = \frac{3}{4}x - \frac{3}{10}x = \frac{9}{20}x$. We can divide the equations for S and T

by each other to solve for S in terms of T:

$$\frac{S = \frac{1}{4}x}{T = \frac{9}{20}x} \qquad \frac{S}{T} = \frac{5}{9}$$

$$\frac{S}{T} = \frac{\frac{5}{20}x}{\frac{9}{20}x} \qquad S = \frac{5}{9}T$$

Chapter 8
of

EQUATIONS, INEQUALITIES, & VICs

STRATEGIES FOR
DATA SUFFICIENCY

In This Chapter . . .

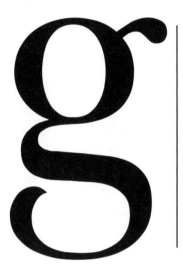

- Rephrasing: MADS Manipulations
- Sample Rephrasings for Challenging Problems

Rephrasing: MADS Manipulations

Data sufficiency problems that involve algebraic equations and inequalities can usually be solved through algebraic manipulations, such as the ones we have covered in this strategy guide. In some cases, you will need to manipulate the original question; in others, you will need to manipulate the statements. Sometimes, you will need to manipulate both.

Remember, the major manipulations include the following:

Multiplication and division by some number
Addition and subtraction
Distributing and factoring
Squaring and unsquaring

Remember the four
MADS manipulations.

You can also consider combination and substitution as manipulations for combining two or more equations. Likewise, combining inequalities is also a manipulation. When you use manipulations to rephrase, you will often uncover very simple questions that have been disguised by the GMAT writers to look complicated.

Is $p > q$?

(1) $-3p < -3q$
(2) $p - r > q - r$

(A) Statement (1) ALONE is sufficient, but statement (2) alone is not sufficient.
(B) Statement (2) ALONE is sufficient, but statement (1) alone is not sufficient.
(C) BOTH statements TOGETHER are sufficient, but NEITHER statement ALONE is sufficient.
(D) EACH statement ALONE is sufficient.
(E) Statements (1) and (2) together are NOT sufficient.

You can rephrase both statements by performing simple manipulations.

Rephrase statement (1) by dividing both sides by -3. The result is $p > q$, since you must switch the direction of an inequality when dividing by a negative number.

Rephrase statement (2) by adding r to both sides. The result is $p > q$.

Now this question is simply: Is $p > q$?

(1) $p > q$
(2) $p > q$

Clearly, either statement is sufficient to answer the question, since the rephrased statements match the question exactly. The answer to this data sufficiency problem is **(D)**: EACH statement ALONE is sufficient.

*Manhattan*GMAT*Prep
the new standard

Sometimes, rephrasing a statement may not uncover the answer to the question itself, but doing so may get you closer to the information that you need to answer the question.

Consider this example:

What is the value of $r + u$?

   (1) $rs - ut = 8 + rt - us$
   (2) $s - t = 6$

As you rephrase, always keep in mind the variable or variable combo you are trying to isolate. This can help you manipulate equations and inequalities. In order to determine the value of the variable combo $r + u$, we will need to isolate $r + u$ on one side of an equation.

Manipulate statement (1) by moving all the variables to one side and factoring out common terms.

$$rs - rt + us - ut = 8$$
$$r(s - t) + u(s - t) = 8$$
$$(r + u)(s - t) = 8$$

$$r + u = \frac{8}{s - t}$$

We have manipulated statement (1) so that $r + u$ is isolated. Although we still do not have a value for $r + u$, the information uncovered by this manipulation becomes important once we look at statement (2).

On its own, statement (2) is insufficient because it tells us nothing about the value of $r + u$. It simply tells us that $s - t = 6$.

However, when we look at both statements together, we can plug the value of $s - t$ provided by statement (2) into our rephrased statement (1) to get a value for $r + u$.

$$r + u = \frac{8}{s - t} = \frac{8}{6}$$

The answer to this data sufficiency problem is **(C)**: BOTH statements TOGETHER are sufficient, but NEITHER statement ALONE is sufficient.

When you see a complicated variable expression in a data sufficiency problem, look for ways to manipulate it.

The combo manipulations you perform may reveal that the underlying variables have more than one value, but you should not stop checking the result. Sometimes, even when the variables have multiple potential values, the answer to the question stays the same.

What is the value of ab^2?

(1) $a = b - 1$
(2) $a = b^2 - 1$

We can pick values for a and b for each statement alone such that we get different values for ab^2. For example, in statement (1), if $a = 2$ and $b = 3$, then $ab^2 = 18$, whereas if $a = 3$ and $b = 4$, then $ab^2 = 48$. In statement (2), if $a = 8$ and $b = 3$, then $ab^2 = 72$, whereas if $a = 3$ and $b = 2$, then $ab^2 = 12$.

If we combine statements (1) and (2), we find that a and b can still have 2 different values:

$$b - 1 = b^2 - 1 \qquad 0 = b(b-1)$$
$$b = b^2 \qquad\qquad b = \{0, 1\}$$
$$0 = b^2 - b \qquad\quad a = \{-1, 0\}$$

So $b = 0$ when $a = -1$, and $b = 1$ when $a = 0$. However in either case, $ab^2 = 0$. Therefore statements (1) and (2) combined are sufficient. The correct answer is **(C)**.

Consider this problem, which involves manipulating statements and then testing numbers.

If $ab = 8$, is a greater than b?

(1) $-3b \geq -18$
(2) $2b \geq 8$

First rephrase statement (1) by manipulating the inequality $-3b \geq -18$.

If you divide both sides of the inequality in statement (1) by -3, you get $b \leq 6$. (Do not forget to flip the direction of the inequality when dividing by a negative number.)

You can test numbers to see whether $b \leq 6$ determines whether a is greater than b.

If $b = 2$, then $a = 4$, in which case a IS greater than b. However, if $b = 4$, then $a = 2$, in which case a is NOT greater than b. Thus, statement (1) is NOT sufficient to answer the question.

Next, rephrase statement (2) by manipulating the inequality $2b \geq 8$. Divide both sides of the inequality by 2 to get $b \geq 4$. Given that b is positive, a must be positive (since we are told that the product ab is positive). The smallest possible value for b is 4, which would mean that a is 2. All other possible values for b are greater than 4, and so the corresponding values for a would be less than 2.

Therefore, statement (2) IS sufficient to answer the question: a is NOT greater than b. The correct answer is **(B)**.

When solving a combo problem, do not stop solving even if some variables can take on multiple values.

*Manhattan*GMAT*Prep
the new standard

Frequently on the GMAT, combos are "hidden": that is, they are not asked about directly. In these cases, you must rephrase the question to find the hidden combo in that case.

Consider this sample question:

If $x + 2z = 3y$, what is x?

Since we are asked about x, we should rephrase the question by solving for x:

$x = 3y - 2z$

Because the GMAT is unlikely to give us the value of x directly, we can rephrase the question to: "What is $3y - 2z$"?

Finally, be on the lookout for hidden meaning in certain statements as you rephrase a question. Sometimes a particular piece of information has an intuitive interpretation that you will not see by simply plodding through the algebra. Consider this example:

Is $xy = -1$?

(1) $x = y$
(2) $y = 1$

At first glance it would seem that we need both statements (1) and (2) to solve the problem: by combining the statements, we see that $x = y = 1$, so $xy = 1$, and the answer to the question is that xy does NOT equal -1. However, upon closer inspection, you should see that only statement (1) is needed. If $x = y$, then the question can be rephrased thus:

Is $x^2 = -1$?

The answer to this question is NO, because squared terms cannot be negative. The correct answer is **(A)**.

Rephrasing: Challenge Short Set

In Chapters 9 and 14, you will find lists of Equations, Inequalities, and VIC problems that have appeared on past official GMAT exams. These lists refer to problems from three books published by the Graduate Management Admission Council® (the organization that develops the official GMAT exam):

The Official Guide for GMAT Review, 12th Edition
The Official Guide for GMAT Quantitative Review
The Official Guide for GMAT Quantitative Review, 2nd Edition

Note: The two editions of the Quant Review book largely overlap. Use one OR the other. The questions contained in these three books are the property of The Graduate Management Admission Council, which is not affiliated in any way with Manhattan GMAT.

As you work through the Data Sufficiency problems listed at the end of Part I and Part II, be sure to focus on *rephrasing*. If possible, try to *rephrase* each question into its simplest form *before* looking at the two statements. In order to rephrase, focus on figuring out the specific information that is absolutely necessary to answer the question. After rephrasing the question, you should also try to *rephrase* each of the two statements, if possible. Rephrase each statement by simplifying the given information into its most basic form.

In order to help you practice rephrasing, we have taken a set of generally difficult Data Sufficiency problems on *The Official Guide* problem list (these are the problem numbers listed in the "Challenge Short Set" on page 205) and have provided you with our own sample rephrasings for each question and statement. In order to evaluate how effectively you are using the rephrasing strategy, you can compare your rephrased questions and statements to our own rephrasings that appear below. Questions and statements that are significantly rephrased appear in **bold**.

Rephrasings from *The Official Guide For GMAT Review, 12th Edition*

The questions and statements that appear below are only our *rephrasings*. The original questions and statements can be found by referencing the problem numbers below in the Data Sufficiency section of *The Official Guide for GMAT Review, 12th edition* (pages 272–288).

Note: Problem numbers preceded by "D" refer to questions in the Diagnostic Test chapter of *The Official Guide for GMAT Review, 12th edition* (pages 24–26).

26. $\dfrac{900}{1 + c2^{-6}} = ?$

What is c?

(1) $180 = \dfrac{900}{1 + c2^{-1}}$

(2) $300 = \dfrac{900}{1 + c2^{-2}}$

30.   What is the value of n?

(1) $n^2 + n = 6$
        $n^2 + n - 6 = 0$
        $(n + 3)(n - 2) = 0$ $n = \{-3, 2\}$

(2) $2^{2n} = 16$
     $2^{2n} = 2^4$
     $2n = 4$ $n = 2$

38. $\dfrac{p_1}{r_1} > \dfrac{p_2}{r_2}$?

$p_1 r_2 > p_2 r_1$?   Note that all variables are positive.

(1) $p_1 > p_2$

(2) $r_2 > r_1$

45.   What is the largest n such that $rn < 100$?
        What is r?

(1) $r \times 50 = 500$

(2) $r \times 100 + r \times 105 = 2{,}050$

the new standard

80.   Is $r^2 < s^2$?

     Is $r < s$?   Note that both variables are positive.

         (1) $r = \dfrac{3}{4}s$

         (2) $s = r + 4$

97.   No rephrasing is necessary.

         (1) $x > 3$ or $x < -3$

             Since x is negative, **$x < -3$**

         (2) $x < \sqrt[3]{-9} \approx -2.1$

115.   Min$(10, w) = $?

     Is $w < 10$, and if so, what is w?

         (1) $w \geq 20$

         (2) $w \geq 10$

125.   **Does ∘ mean multiplication?**

         (1) ∘ means subtraction

         (2) No rephrasing necessary

154.   Is $b - a \geq 2(3^n - 2^n)$?

         (1) $b - a = 3^{n+1} - 2^{n+1}$

             $b - a = (3)3^n - (2)2^n$

             $b - a \geq (2)3^n - (2)2^n$

         (2) No meaningful rephrasing can be done here. No information is given about a or b.

156.   **Is $5^k < 1000$?**

         (1) $5^{k+1} > 3000$

           $5\left(5^k\right) > 3000$

              $5^k > 600$

         (2) $5^k - 5^{k-1} = 500$

            $5^k(1 - 5^{-1}) = 500$

           $5^k(1 - 1/5) = 500$

              $5^k(4/5) = 500$

                $5^k = 500(5/4)$

                $5^k = 625$

158.   Let m = the number of members
Let d = the dollar amount contributed by each member
$md = 60$
What is m?

(1) $d = 4$

(2) $(m - 5)(d + 2) = 60$

Substitute from the question: $d = \dfrac{60}{m}$

$(m - 5)(\dfrac{60}{m} + 2) = 60$

$m^2 - 5m - 150 = 0$
$(m - 15)(m + 10) = 0$
$m = -10$ or 15, but the number of members cannot be negative, so $\boldsymbol{m = 15}$.

162.   Is $n + k > 4n$?
Is $\boldsymbol{k > 3n}$?

(1) $k > 3n$
(2) $k > 2n$

168. $\dfrac{3t - x}{t - x} = ?$

Now, either stop here or divide top and bottom by t:

$\dfrac{3 - x/t}{1 - x/t} = ?$

What is the value of $\dfrac{x}{t}$?

(1) $2t = 3t - 3x$

$-t = -3x$

$\dfrac{x}{t} = \dfrac{1}{3}$

(2) $t = x + 5$

$t - 5 = x$

$\dfrac{x}{t} = \dfrac{t - 5}{t}$

D30.   Let x = number of $100 certificates sold
$20 - x$ = number of $10 certificates sold
What is $20 - x$? OR What is x?

(1) $1650 < 100x + 10(20 - x) < 1800$
$1450 < 90x < 1600$

$16\dfrac{1}{9} < x < 17\dfrac{7}{9}$

Since x is a whole number, $x = 17$.

(2) $x > 15$

D33.   Is $\dfrac{5^{x+2}}{25} < 1$?

For this to be less than 1, the numerator 5^{x+2} must be less than the denominator.
Is $5^{x+2} < 25$?
Is $5^{x+2} < 5^2$?

Is $x + 2 < 2$?
Is $x < 0$?

(1) $x < 0$

(2) $x < 0$

Rephrasings from *The Official Guide for GMAT Quantitative Review, 2nd Edition*

The questions and statements that appear below are only our *rephrasings*. The original questions and statements can be found by referencing the problem numbers below in the Data Sufficiency section of *The Official Guide for GMAT Quantitative Review, 2nd Edition* (pages 152–163). First Edition numbers are included in parentheses. Problems unique to one edition are so indicated.

89.   No meaningful rephrasing can be done here. Combining inequalities by addition is the best way to
(85.)   solve this problem (if $a > b$ and $c > d$, then $a + c > b + d$).

121.   Is $(x)^y < (y)^x$?
(115.)

In this problem, rephrase the inequality in the question by plugging in the information provided in statement (1).

(1) $x = y^2$
   Is $(y^2)^y < (y)^{y^2}$?
   Is $y^{2y} < y^{y^2}$?

Now, drop the base (y) and compare the exponents on either side of the inequality. Since this is an inequality, we have to analyze this for three cases: when y is greater than 1, when y is between 1 and 0, and when y is negative.

For y > 1: Is $2y < y^2$? This is true only if $y > 2$.

Is $y > 2$?

For 0 < y < 1: Is $2y > y^2$? This becomes "Is $2 > y$?" This is true for all numbers in the range between 0 and 1.

For y < 0: The question cannot be easily rephrased.

However, the $y > 1$ scenario is enough to show that statement (1) is insufficient since y might not be greater than 2. (Incidentally, if we considered the border case $y = 1$, then we would get $x = 1^2 = 1$ and the question would be answered No.)

(2) $y > 2$

No information is given about x. Test numbers to see that this information does not yield a conclusive YES or NO answer.

(COMBINED) The rephrased question from the first statement (Is $y > 2$?) is answered by the information provided in the second statement ($y > 2$). (We do not need to analyze the cases in which $y < 1$, since the information provided in the second statement eliminates the possibility that y is less than 1.)

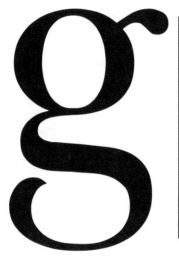

Chapter 9
of
EQUATIONS, INEQUALITIES, & VICs

OFFICIAL GUIDE PROBLEM SETS: PART I

In This Chapter . . .

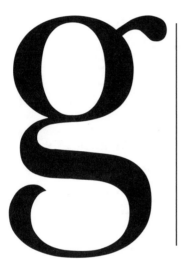

- Equations, Inequalities, & VICs Problem Solving List from *The Official Guides:* PART I
- Equations, Inequalities, & VICs Data Sufficiency List from *The Official Guides:* PART I

Practicing with REAL GMAT Problems

Now that you have completed Part I of *EQUATIONS, INEQUALITIES, & VICs* it is time to test your skills on problems that have actually appeared on real GMAT exams over the past several years.

The problem sets that follow are composed of questions from three books published by the Graduate Management Admission Council® (the organization that develops the official GMAT exam):

The Official Guide for GMAT Review, 12th Edition
The Official Guide for GMAT Quantitative Review
The Official Guide for GMAT Quantitative Review, 2nd Edition
Note: The two editions of the Quant Review book largely overlap. Use one OR the other.

These books contain quantitative questions that have appeared on past official GMAT exams. (The questions contained therein are the property of The Graduate Management Admission Council, which is not affiliated in any way with Manhattan GMAT.)

Although the questions in the Official Guides have been "retired" (they will not appear on future official GMAT exams), they are great practice questions.

In order to help you practice effectively, we have categorized every problem in The Official Guides by topic and subtopic. On the following pages, you will find two categorized lists:

(1) **Problem Solving:** Lists EASIER Problem Solving Equations, Inequalities, & VIC questions contained in *The Official Guides* and categorizes them by subtopic.

(2) **Data Sufficiency:** Lists EASIER Data Sufficiency Equations, Inequalities, & VIC questions contained in *The Official Guides* and categorizes them by subtopic.

The remaining *Official Guide* problems are listed at the end of Part II of this book. **Do not forget about the Part II list!**

Each book in Manhattan GMAT's 8-book strategy series contains its own *Official Guide* lists that pertain to the specific topic of that particular book. If you complete all the practice problems contained on the *Official Guide* lists in each of the 8 Manhattan GMAT preparation books, you will have completed every single question published in *The Official Guides*.

Problem Solving: Part I

from *The Official Guide for GMAT Review, 12th Edition* (pages 20–23 & 152–185), *The Official Guide for GMAT Quantitative Review* (pages 62–85), and *The Official Guide for GMAT Quantitative Review, 2nd Edition* (pages 62–86).

<u>Note</u>: The two editions of the Quant Review book largely overlap. Use one OR the other.

Solve each of the following problems in a notebook, making sure to demonstrate how you arrived at each answer by showing all of your work and computations. If you get stuck on a problem, look back at the EQUATIONS, INEQUALITIES, and VICs strategies and content contained in this guide to assist you.

<u>Note</u>: Problem numbers preceded by "D" refer to questions in the Diagnostic Test chapter of *The Official Guide for GMAT Review, 12th edition* (pages 20–23).

GENERAL SET – EQUATIONS, INEQUALITIES, & VICs

Basic Equations

> *12th Edition*: 2, 38, 44, 58, 70, 100, 168
> *Quantitative Review*: 38, 68, 107 OR *2nd Edition*: 2, 40, 41, 107

Equations with Exponents

> *12th Edition*: 104
> *Quantitative Review*: 7, 72, 75, 96, 106 OR *2nd Edition*: 74, 96, 106

Quadratic Equations

> *12th Edition*: 41, 97, 144, 155, D16
> *Quantitative Review*: 18, 55, 58, 86 OR *2nd Edition*: 20, 57, 72, 103

Formulas & Functions

> *12th Edition*: 42, 68, 98, 136, 188, D3
> *Quantitative Review*: 26, 78, 91, 113, 144 OR *2nd Edition*: 1, 28, 77, 91, 113, 144

Inequalities

> *12th Edition*: 49, 71, 119, 125, 130
> *Quantitative Review*: 3, 83, 92 OR *2nd Edition*: 5, 92

VICs

> *12th Edition*: 6, 31, 34, 84, 89, 112, 120, 122, 127, 158, D24
> *Quantitative Review*: 1, 29, 32, 42, 52, 60, 69, 85, 99, 104, 111, 115, 116
> OR *2nd Edition*: 3, 31, 34, 44, 54, 85, 99, 104, 111, 115, 116

Remember, there are more Official Guide problems listed at the end of Part II.

Data Sufficiency: Part I

from *The Official Guide for GMAT Review, 12th Edition* (pages 24–26 & 272–288), *The Official Guide for GMAT Quantitative Review* (pages 149–157), and *The Official Guide for GMAT Quantitative Review, 2nd Edition* (pages 152–163).

Note: The two editions of the Quant Review book largely overlap. Use one OR the other.

Solve each of the following problems in a notebook, making sure to demonstrate how you arrived at each answer by showing all of your work and computations. If you get stuck on a problem, look back at the EQUATIONS, INEQUALITIES, AND VICs strategies and content contained in this guide to assist you.

Practice REPHRASING both the questions and the statements by manipulating equations and inequalities. The majority of data sufficiency problems can be rephrased; however, if you have difficulty rephrasing a problem, try testing numbers to solve it. It is especially important that you familiarize yourself with the directions for data sufficiency problems, and that you memorize the 5 fixed answer choices that accompany all data sufficiency problems.

Note: Problem numbers preceded by "D" refer to questions in the Diagnostic Test chapter of *The Official Guide for GMAT Review, 12th edition* (pages 24–26).

GENERAL SET – EQUATIONS, INEQUALITIES, & VICs

Basic Equations
12th Edition: 1, 15, 35, 60, 83, D35
Quantitative Review: 6, 15, 21, 23, 35, 56, 60, 77, 90
OR *2nd Edition*: 57, 61, 80, 94

Equations with Exponents
12th Edition: 154, 156
Quantitative Review: 9, 25, 28, 96 OR *2nd Edition*: 100

Quadratic Equations
12th Edition: 30
Quantitative Review: 37, 46, 61 OR *2nd Edition*: 46, 62, 73

Formulas & Functions
12th Edition: 19, 26, 36, 45
Quantitative Review: 68

Inequalities
12th Edition: 11, 38, 49, 51, 72, 80, D30, D33
Quantitative Review: 32, 40, 42, 43, 51, 55
OR *2nd Edition*: 40, 42, 51, 52, 56

Remember, there are more Official Guide problems listed at the end of Part II.

PART II: ADVANCED

This part of the book covers various advanced topics within *Equations, Inequalities and VICs*. This advanced material may not be necessary for all students. Attempt Part II only if you have completed Part I and are comfortable with its content.

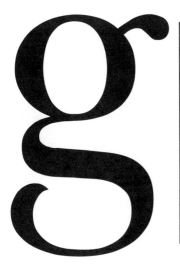

Chapter 10
of
EQUATIONS, INEQUALITIES, & VICs

EQUATIONS: ADVANCED

In This Chapter . . .

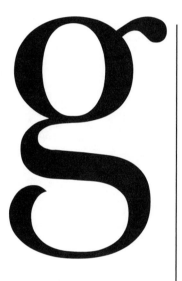

- Complex Absolute Value Equations
- Integer Constraints
- Advanced Algebraic Techniques
- Advanced Quadratic Techniques

Complex Absolute Value Equations

So far we have only looked at absolute value equations that have one unknown inside one absolute value expression. However, these equations can get more complicated by including more than one absolute value expression. There are two primary types of these <u>complex</u> absolute value equations:

(1) The equation contains TWO or more variables in more than one absolute value expression. These equations, which usually lack constants, are generally NOT easy to solve with algebra. Instead, a conceptual approach is preferable. Problems of this type are discussed in the "Positives & Negatives Strategy" chapter of the Manhattan GMAT *Number Properties* Strategy Guide.

(2) The equation contains ONE variable and at least one CONSTANT in more than one absolute value expression. These equations are usually easier to solve with an algebraic approach than with a conceptual approach. For example:

> If $|x - 2| = |2x - 3|$, what are the possible values for x?

We have one variable (x) and three constants (-2, 2 and -3). Thus we know that we should take an algebraic approach to the problem.

Because there are two absolute value expressions, each of which yields two algebraic cases, it seems that we need to test *four* cases overall: positive/positive, positive/negative, negative/positive, and negative/negative.

> (1) The positive/positive case: $(x - 2) = (2x - 3)$
> (2) The positive/negative case: $(x - 2) = -(2x - 3)$
> (3) The negative/positive case: $-(x - 2) = (2x - 3)$
> (4) The negative/negative case: $-(x - 2) = -(2x - 3)$

However, note that case (1) and case (4) yield the same equation. Likewise, case (2) and case (3) yield the same equation. Thus, you only need to consider two real cases: one in which neither expression changes sign, and another in which one expression changes sign.

<table>
<tr><td><u>CASE A: Same sign</u></td><td><u>CASE B: Different signs</u></td></tr>
<tr><td>$(x - 2) = (2x - 3)$</td><td>$(x - 2) = -(2x - 3)$</td></tr>
<tr><td>$1 = x$</td><td>$3x = 5$</td></tr>
<tr><td></td><td>$x = \dfrac{5}{3}$</td></tr>
</table>

We also have to check the validity of the solutions once we have solved the equations.

Both solutions are valid, because $|1 - 2| = |2(1) - 3| = 1$, and $\left|\dfrac{5}{3} - 2\right| = \left|2\left(\dfrac{5}{3}\right) - 3\right| = \dfrac{1}{3}$.

> When you have an equation with *one* variable in more than one absolute value expression, you should probably take an algebraic approach.

Integer Constraints

Occasionally, a GMAT algebra problem contains integer constraints. In such a case, there might be many possible solutions among *all* numbers but only one <u>integer</u> solution.

> $2y - x = 2xy$ and $x \neq 0$. If x and y are integers, which of the following could equal y?
>
> (A) 2
> (B) 1
> (C) 0
> (D) −1
> (E) −2

First, we solve for x in terms of y, so that we can test values of y in the answer choices.

$$2y - x = 2xy \qquad 2y = 2xy + x \qquad 2y = x(2y + 1) \qquad x = \frac{2y}{2y + 1}$$

> *When you have integer constraints on solutions, solve for one variable and then test numbers.*

Ordinarily, this result would not be enough for us to reach an answer. However, we know that both x and y must be integers. Therefore, we should find which integer value of y generates an integer value for x.

Now, we test the possibilities for y, using the answer choices. The case $y = 0$ produces $x = 0$, but this outcome is disallowed by the condition that $x \neq 0$. The only other case that produces an integer value for x is $y = -1$, yielding $x = 2$. Thus, the answer is (**D**). Integer constraints together with <u>inequalities</u> can also lead to just one solution.

> If x and y are nonnegative integers and $x + y = 25$, what is x?
>
> (1) $20x + 10y < 300$
> (2) $20x + 10y > 280$

First, we should note that since x and y must be positive integers, the smallest possible value for $20x + 10y$ is 250, when $x = 0$ and $y = 25$. Statement (1) does not tell us what x is, nor does statement (2). However, if we combine the statements, we get:

$$280 < 20x + 10y < 300$$

Substituting ($25 \div x$) for y:
$$280 < 20x + 10(25 - x) < 300$$
$$280 < 20x + 250 - 10x < 300$$
$$30 < 10x < 50$$
$$3 < x < 5$$

Since x must be an integer, x must equal 4. Therefore the answer is (**C**): Statements 1 and 2 TOGETHER are sufficient. (Incidentally, if we relax the integer constraint, x can be any real number that is more than 3 and less than 5.)

Advanced Algebraic Techniques

MULTIPLYING OR DIVIDING TWO EQUATIONS

A general rule of thumb in algebra is that you can do just about anything you want to one side of an equation, as long as you do the same thing to the other side (except divide or multiply by 0). Thus, **you can multiply or divide two complete equations together, because when you do so, you are doing the same thing to both sides of the equation—** by definition, both sides of an equation are equal.

What does it mean to multiply two equations together? It means that you multiply the left sides of the two equations together, and also multiply the right sides of the equations together. You then set those products equal to each other. To divide two equations, you take the same kinds of steps.

> Multiply or divide two equations when it seems that you can cancel a lot of variables in one move.

If $xy^2 = -96$ and $\dfrac{1}{xy} = \dfrac{1}{24}$, what is y?

While we could calculate the individual variables by solving for x or y first and substituting, if we simply multiply the equations together, we will quickly see that $y = -4$:

$$xy^2 \left(\frac{1}{xy} \right) = -96 \left(\frac{1}{24} \right) \qquad \frac{xy^2}{xy} = \frac{-96}{24} \qquad y = -4$$

If $\dfrac{a}{b} = 16$ and $\dfrac{a}{b^2} = 8$, what is ab?

Again, we could calculate the individual variables by solving for a first and substituting. But if we simply divide the first equation by the second, we will quickly see that $b = 2$:

$$\frac{\dfrac{a}{b}}{\dfrac{a}{b^2}} = \frac{16}{8} \qquad \frac{b^2 a}{ba} = 2 \qquad b = 2$$

We can then solve for a, and find that $ab = 64$:

$$\frac{a}{2} = 16 \qquad a = 16(2) = 32 \qquad ab = 32(2) = 64$$

EQUATIONS: ADVANCED STRATEGY

ADVANCED FACTORING & DISTRIBUTING

GMAT problems often contain expressions that can be presented in factored form or distributed form. Distributing a factored expression or factoring a distributed expression can often help the solution process. A general rule of thumb is that **when you encounter any expression or equation in which two or more terms include the same variable, you should consider factoring as an approach.** Similarly, **when an expression is given in factored form, consider distributing it.**

Factoring or distributing may be beneficial in various situations. It is especially important to note that you should feel comfortable going both ways: from distributed form to factored form, and vice versa. Here are some examples:

Be ready to switch between the distributed and the factored form of any expression.

DISTRIBUTED FORM		FACTORED FORM
$x^2 + x$	$\longleftrightarrow$	$x(x+1)$
$x^5 - x^3$	$\longleftrightarrow$	$x^3(x^2-1) = x^3(x+1)(x-1)$
$6^5 - 6^3$	$\longleftrightarrow$	$6^3(6^2-1) = 35 \cdot 6^3$
$4^8 + 4^9 + 4^{10}$	$\longleftrightarrow$	$4^8(1+4+4^2) = 21 \cdot 4^8$
$p^3 - p$	$\longleftrightarrow$	$p(p^2-1) = p(p+1)(p-1)$
$a^b + a^{b+1}$	$\longleftrightarrow$	$a^b(1+a)$
$3^5 + 3^6$		$3^5(1+3)$
$m^n - m^{n-1}$	$\longleftrightarrow$	$m^n(1-m^{-1}) = m^{n-1}(m-1)$
$5^5 - 5^4$		$5^5(1-\frac{1}{5}) = 5^4(5-1)$
$xw + yw + zx + zy$	$\longleftrightarrow$	$w(x+y) + z(x+y) =$
		$(w+z)(x+y)$

If you have trouble seeing how one form translates into the other, you should practice both recognizing and manipulating in both directions.

Advanced Quadratic Techniques

TAKING THE SQUARE ROOT

So far we have seen how to solve quadratic equations by setting one side of the equation equal to zero and factoring. However, some quadratic problems can be solved without setting one side equal to zero. If the other side of the equation is a **perfect square** quadratic, the problem can be quickly solved by taking the square root of both sides of the equation.

> If $(z+3)^2 = 25$, what is z?

We could solve this problem by distributing the left-hand side of the equation, setting the right-hand side equal to zero, and factoring. However, it would be much easier to simply take the square root of both sides of the equation to solve for z. You just have to consider both the positive and the negative square root.

$$\sqrt{(z+3)^2} = \sqrt{25}$$

Note that square-rooting the square of something is the same as taking the absolute value of that thing.

$$|z+3| = 5$$
$$z + 3 = \pm 5$$
$$z = -3 \pm 5$$
$$z = \{2, -8\}$$

Any quadratic that can be solved by taking the square root of both sides SHOULD be solved that way.

SUBSTITUTING

Very occasionally, you might substitute a variable to create a quadratic.

> Given that $x^4 - 5x^2 + 4 = 0$, what is NOT a possible value of x?
> (A) −2   (B) −1   (C) 0   (D) 1   (E) 2

We have a fourth power, a second power, and a constant term. This equation does not look like a quadratic, but we can convert it to a quadratic if we make the following substitution: $z = x^2$. This transforms the equation as follows:

$$z^2 - 5z + 4 = 0$$
$$(z-4)(z-1) = 0$$

Thus, $z = 4$ OR $z = 1$. Now switch back to x: $x^2 = 4$ OR $x^2 = 1$. Therefore, $x = \pm 2$ OR $x = \pm 1$.

The only value among the answer choices NOT listed is 0. The correct answer is (C). We could also have plugged in the answer choices and quickly seen that 0 would not work in the original equation.

QUADRATIC FORMULA

The vast majority of quadratic equations on the GMAT can be solved by the factoring or square-rooting techniques described in this chapter. However, very occasionally you might encounter a problem difficult to solve with these techniques. Such a problem requires an understanding of the quadratic formula, which can solve any quadratic equation but is cumbersome to use.

Quadratic Formula: **For any quadratic equation of the form $ax^2 + bx + c = 0$, where a, b, and c are constants, the solutions for x are given by:**

$$x = \frac{-b \pm \sqrt{b^2 - 4ac}}{2a}$$

Consider: If $x^2 + 8x + 13 = 0$, what is x?

This problem cannot be factored because there are no two integers for which the sum is 8 and the product is 13. However, we can find the solutions simply by plugging the coefficients from the equation into the quadratic formula:

$$x = \frac{-8 \pm \sqrt{8^2 - 4(1)(13)}}{2(1)} = \frac{-8 \pm \sqrt{64 - 52}}{2(1)} = -4 \pm \frac{\sqrt{12}}{2} = \{-4 + \sqrt{3}, -4 - \sqrt{3}\}$$

It is not imperative that you memorize the quadratic formula, but the expression underneath the radical in the formula (called the **discriminant**) can convey important information: it can tell you how many solutions the equation has. If the discriminant is **greater than** zero, there will be two solutions. If the discriminant is **equal to** zero, there will be one solution. If the discriminant is **less than** zero, there will be **no** solutions, because you cannot take the square root of a negative number.

> Which of the following equations has no solution for x?
>
> (A) $x^2 - 8x - 11 = 0$
> (B) $x^2 + 8x + 11 = 0$
> (C) $x^2 + 7x + 11 = 0$
> (D) $x^2 - 6x + 11 = 0$
> (E) $x^2 - 6x - 11 = 0$

None of these equations can be solved by factoring. However, we can determine which of the equations has no solution by determining which equation has a negative discriminant:

> (A) $b^2 - 4ac = (-8)^2 - 4(1)(-11) = 64 + 44 = 108$
> (B) $b^2 - 4ac = (8)^2 - 4(1)(11) = 64 - 44 = 20$
> (C) $b^2 - 4ac = (7)^2 - 4(1)(11) = 49 - 44 = 5$
> (D) $b^2 - 4ac = (-6)^2 - 4(1)(11) = 36 - 44 = \mathbf{-8}$
> (E) $b^2 - 4ac = (-6)^2 - 4(1)(-11) = 36 + 44 = 80$

Therefore the equation in answer choice **(D)** has no solution. Again, **it is very rare for a GMAT problem to require familiarity with the quadratic formula.** The vast majority of quadratic equations can be factored through conventional methods.

*Manhattan*GMAT*Prep
the new standard

Use the discriminant of the quadratic formula to determine how many solutions a difficult quadratic equation has.

Problem Set (Advanced)

Solve each problem, applying the concepts and rules you learned in this section.

1. Given that $|6 + x| = 2x + 1$, what is x?

2. Given that $x - y = 3$, $y - z = 2$, and $x + z = 7$, what is y?

3. Given that $5x + 9y + 4 = 2x + 3y + 31$, what is $x + 2y$?

4. Given that $\dfrac{zx + zy}{9} = 4$ and $x + y = 3$, what is z?

5. Given that $ab = 12$ and $\dfrac{c}{a} + 10 = 15$, what is bc?

6. If $|x + 1| = |3x - 2|$, what are the possible values for x?

    (A) 1/4 and 3/4
    (B) 1/4 and 3/2
    (C) 2/3 and 3/2
    (D) 2/3 and 4/3
    (E) 3/4 and 4/3

7. If $xy = 2$, $xz = 8$, and $yz = 5$, then the value of xyz is closest to

    (A) 5
    (B) 9
    (C) 15
    (D) 25
    (E) 75

8. If $c + d = 11$ and c and d are positive integers, which of the following is a possible value for $5c + 8d$?

    (A) 55
    (B) 61
    (C) 69
    (D) 83
    (E) 88

9. If $mn = 3(m + 1) + n$ and m and n are integers, m could be any of the following values EXCEPT:

    (A) 2
    (B) 3
    (C) 4
    (D) 5
    (E) 7

For #10–11, write the expression in factored form (if distributed) and in distributed form (if factored):

10. $x^{a+3} - x^a$

11. $n^2(n+1)(n-1)$

12.   Given that $\dfrac{x^3 + 4x^2 + 4x}{x} = 9$, what is x?

13.   Given that $(t+1)^2 = 18$, what is t?

14.   Given that $(p-3)^2 - 5 = 0$, what is p?

15.   Given that $z^2 - 10z + 25 = 9$, what is z?

16.   Given that $x^4 - 13x^2 + 36 = 0$, what is x?

17.   Which of the following equations has no solution for a?

   (A) $a^2 - 6a + 7 = 0$
   (B) $a^2 + 6a - 7 = 0$
   (C) $a^2 + 4a + 3 = 0$
   (D) $a^2 - 4a + 3 = 0$
   (E) $a^2 - 4a + 5 = 0$

1. $x = 5$:

$$|6 + x| = 2x + 1$$

First, isolate the expression within the absolute value brackets. Then, solve for two cases, one in which the expression is positive and one in which it is negative. Finally, test the validity of your solutions. Note that Case 2 is not valid here.

Case 1: $6 + x = 2x + 1$ Case 2: $6 + x = -(2x + 1)$
            $5 = x$ $6 + x = -2x - 1$
                                      $3x = -7$

$$x = -\frac{7}{3}$$

Case 1 is valid because $|6 + 5| = 11$ and $2(5) + 1 = 11$.

Case 2 is NOT valid because $\left|6 - \dfrac{7}{3}\right| = \dfrac{11}{3}$, but $2\left(-\dfrac{7}{3}\right) + 1 = -\dfrac{11}{3}$.

2. **3:** This problem contains 3 variables and 3 equations. Look for a way to add up all the equations, cancelling variables as you go.

If you simply add all the equations as given, you cancel the y terms and the z terms. Line up the variables as shown:

$$
\begin{array}{rrrl}
x & - y & & = 3 \\
 & y & - z & = 2 \\
x & & + z & = 7 \\
\hline
2x & & & = 12 \\
 & & x & = 6
\end{array}
$$

Substituting this result back into the first equation ($x - y = 3$), we get $y = 3$.

Alternatively, you could reverse the signs on the first equation to make x negative (so it cancels) and y positive (so it does not cancel):

$$
\begin{array}{rrrl}
-x & + y & & = -3 \\
 & y & - z & = 2 \\
x & & + z & = 7 \\
\hline
 & 2y & & = 6 \\
 & y & & = 3
\end{array}
$$

3. $x + 2y = 9$:

$$5x + 9y + 4 = 2x + 3y + 31$$
$$3x + 6y = 27$$
$$3(x + 2y) = 27$$
$$x + 2y = 9$$

4. $z = 12$:

$$\frac{zx + zy}{9} = 4 \qquad x + y = 3$$

$$z(x + y) = 36$$
$$3z = 36$$
$$z = 12$$

We can factor out the z in the left-hand side of the equation and substitute 3 for the combo $x + y$.

5. $bc = 60$:

We can first solve for $\dfrac{c}{a}$, then multiply the two equations together to quickly solve for bc.

$$\frac{c}{a} = 15 - 10 = 5$$

$$(\cancel{a}b)\left(\frac{c}{\cancel{a}}\right) = 12(5) \qquad bc = 12(5) = 60$$

6. (B): 1/4 and 3/2: This is a complex absolute value problem, so we first must decide on an approach. The equation $|x+1| = |3x - 2|$ has one variable (x) and several constants (1, 3, and −2). Thus, we should take an algebraic approach.

In theory, with two absolute value expressions we would set up four cases. However, those four cases collapse to just two cases: (1) the two expressions inside the absolute value symbols are given the same sign, and (2) the two expressions are given the opposite sign.

Case (1): Same Sign	Case (2): Opposite Sign
$x + 1 = 3x - 2$	$x + 1 = -(3x - 2) = -3x + 2$
$3 = 2x$	$4x = 1$
$x = \dfrac{3}{2}$	$x = \dfrac{1}{4}$

Testing each solution in the original equation, we verify that both solutions are valid:

$$\left|\frac{3}{2} + 1\right| = \left|3\left(\frac{3}{2}\right) - 2\right| \qquad \left|\frac{1}{4} + 1\right| = \left|3\left(\frac{1}{4}\right) - 2\right|$$

$$\left|\frac{5}{2}\right| = \left|\frac{9}{2} - 2\right| \qquad \left|\frac{5}{4}\right| = \left|\frac{3}{4} - 2\right| = \left|\frac{-5}{4}\right|$$

$$\frac{5}{2} = \frac{5}{2} \qquad \frac{5}{4} = \frac{5}{4}$$

7. (B) 9: Multiplying together all three equations gives $x^2 y^2 z^2 = 80$. As a result, $xyz = \sqrt{80}$, which is very close to $xyz = 9$.

8. (B) 61: Because c and d must be positive integers and $c + d = 11$, there are only ten possible values for $5c + 8d$ (starting with $c = 1$ and $d = 10$, then $c = 2$ and $d = 9$, and so on):

c	d	$5c + 8d$
1	10	85
2	9	82
3	8	79
4	7	76

Note that the smallest value of $5c + 8d$ is 58, where $c = 10$ and $d = 1$, and the largest value is 85.

You can continue to plug values until you find a match to the answer choices. When $c = 9$, $d = 2$ and $5c + 8d = 61$

Alternatively, you can notice that consecutive values of $5c + 8d$ differ by 3. In other words, every possible value of $5c + 8d$ equals a multiple of 3 plus some constant. By inspection, we see that the values of $5c + 8d$ are all one more than a multiple of 3: for instance, the value $82 = 81 + 1$. The only answer choice that equals a multiple of 3 plus 1 is $61 = 60 + 1$.

9. **(D) 5:** First, we need to solve for n. The reason we solve for n is that the answer choices list possible values for m, the <u>other</u> variable. If we solve for n, then we can plug the possible values for m into the formula and see when we get a non-integer for n, since n must be an integer:

$$mn = 3(m+1) + n$$
$$mn - n = 3(m+1)$$
$$n(m-1) = 3(m+1)$$
$$n = \frac{3(m+1)}{(m-1)} \longrightarrow$$

m	$n = \dfrac{3(m+1)}{(m-1)}$
2	$n = \dfrac{3(2+1)}{(2-1)} = 9$
3	$n = \dfrac{3(3+1)}{(3-1)} = 6$
4	$n = \dfrac{3(4+1)}{(4-1)} = 5$
5	$\mathbf{n = \dfrac{3(5+1)}{(5-1)} = \dfrac{18}{4} = \dfrac{9}{2}}$
7	$n = \dfrac{3(7+1)}{(7-1)} = 4$

Only a value of 5 for m does not produce an integer for n.

10. $x^{a+3} - x^a = \boldsymbol{x^a(x^3 - 1)}$

11. $n^2(n+1)(n-1) = n^2(n^2-1) = \boldsymbol{n^4 - n^2}$

12. $\boldsymbol{x = \{-5, 1\}}$:

$$\frac{x^3 + 4x^2 + 4x}{x} = 9$$

$$x^3 + 4x^2 + 4x = 9x$$
$$x^3 + 4x^2 - 5x = 0$$
$$x(x^2 + 4x - 5) = 0$$
$$x(x + 5)(x - 1) = 0$$

$x = 0$ OR $x + 5 = 0$ OR $x - 1 = 0$
                           $x = -5$ $x = 1$

However, the solution $x = 0$ renders the fraction in the original equation undefined, as we know the denominator of the fraction cannot be 0. Therefore, $x = \{-5, 1\}$.

13. $t = \left\{-1+3\sqrt{2}, -1-3\sqrt{2}\right\}$:

$$(t+1)^2 = 18 \qquad\qquad |t+1| = 3\sqrt{2}$$

$$\sqrt{(t+1)^2} = \sqrt{18} \qquad\qquad t = -1 \pm 3\sqrt{2}$$

14. $p = \left\{3+\sqrt{5}, 3-\sqrt{5}\right\}$:

$$(p-3)^2 - 5 = 0 \qquad\qquad |p-3| = \sqrt{5}$$

$$(p-3)^2 = 5 \qquad\qquad p = 3 \pm \sqrt{5}$$

$$\sqrt{(p-3)^2} = \sqrt{5}$$

15. $z = \{2, 8\}$:

$$z^2 - 10z + 25 = 9 \qquad\qquad |z-5| = 3$$

$$(z-5)^2 = 9 \qquad\qquad z = 5 \pm 3$$

$$\sqrt{(z-5)^2} = \sqrt{9} \qquad\qquad z = 8 \text{ or } 2$$

Since we recognize that the left-hand side of the equation is a perfect square quadratic, we will factor the left side of the equation first, instead of trying to set everything equal to zero.

16. $x = \{-3, -2, 2, 3\}$

Substitute: $y = x^2$

$$y^2 - 13y + 36 = 0$$
$$(y-9)(y-4) = 0$$
$$y = 9 \text{ or } y = 4$$

$$x^2 = 9 \text{ or } x^2 = 4$$
$$x = \pm 3 \text{ or } \pm 2$$

17. **(E):** We can determine which of the equations has no solution by determining which equation has a negative discriminant:

(A) $b^2 - 4ac = (-6)^2 - 4(1)(7) = 36 - 28 = 8$
(B) $b^2 - 4ac = (6)^2 - 4(1)(-7) = 36 + 28 = 64$
(C) $b^2 - 4ac = (4)^2 - 4(1)(3) = 16 - 12 = 4$
(D) $b^2 - 4ac = (-4)^2 - 4(1)(3) = 16 - 12 = 4$
(E) $b^2 - 4ac = (-4)^2 - 4(1)(5) = 16 - 20 = -4$

Chapter 11
of
EQUATIONS, INEQUALITITES, & VICs

FORMULAS &
FUNCTIONS:
ADVANCED

In This Chapter . . .

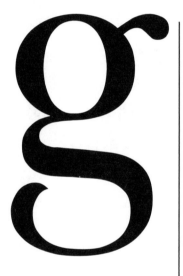

- Recursive Formulas for Sequences
- Advanced Function Types
- Optimization Problems

Recursive Formulas for Sequences

We saw in Part I how a sequence can be defined with a **direct** formula. That is, each term in the sequence is written as a function of n, the term's position in the sequence.

A direct formula looks like this: $A_n = 9n + 3$

If you want to find the value of the one-hundredth term of the sequence, you just plug $n = 100$ into the formula:

$$A_{100} = 9(100) + 3 = 903$$

The GMAT also uses **recursive** formulas to define sequences. With recursive formulas, each item of a sequence is defined in terms of the value of PREVIOUS ITEMS in the sequence.

A recursive formula looks like this: $A_n = A_{n-1} + 9$

This formula simply means "THIS term (A_n) equals the PREVIOUS term (A_{n-1}) plus 9." It is shorthand for a series of specific relationships between successive terms:

$$A_2 = A_1 + 9$$
$$A_3 = A_2 + 9$$
$$A_4 = A_3 + 9, \text{ etc.}$$

> In a recursive formula, the subscript $n-1$ means "the previous term," and the subscript n means "this term."

Whenever you look at a recursive formula, articulate its meaning in words. If necessary, also write out one or two specific relationships that the recursive formula stands for. Think of a recursive formula as a "domino" relationship: if you know A_1, then you can find A_2, and then you can find A_3, then A_4, and so on for all the terms. You can also work backward: if you know A_4, then you can find A_3, A_2, and A_1. However, if you do not know the value of any one term, then you cannot calculate the value of any other. You need one domino to fall, so to speak, in order to knock down all the others.

Thus, to solve for the values of a recursive sequence, you need to be given the recursive rule and ALSO the value of one of the items in the sequence. For example:

$A_n = A_{n-1} + 9$ In this example, A_n is defined in terms of the previous item,
$A_1 = 12$ A_{n-1}. Recall the meaning of this recursive formula: THIS term equals the PREVIOUS term plus 9. Because $A_1 = 12$, we can determine that $A_2 = A_1 + 9 = 12 + 9 = 21$. Therefore, $A_3 = 21 + 9 = 30$, $A_4 = 30 + 9 = 39$, and so on.

Because the first term is 12, this sequence is identical to the sequence defined by the direct definition, $A_n = 9n + 3$, given at the top of this page. Here is another example:

$F_n = F_{n-1} + F_{n-2}$ In this example, F_n is defined in terms of BOTH the previous
$F_1 = 1, F_2 = 1$ item, F_{n-1}, and the item prior to that, F_{n-2}. This recursive formula means "THIS term equals the PREVIOUS term plus the term BEFORE THAT." Because $F_1 = 1$ and $F_2 = 1$, we can determine that $F_3 = F_1 + F_2 = 1 + 1 = 2$. Therefore $F_4 = 2 + 1 = 3$, $F_5 = 3 + 2 = 5$, $F_6 = 5 + 3 = 8$, and so on. There is no simple direct rule for this sequence.

*Manhattan*GMAT*Prep
the new standard

Direct formulas are usually handier than recursive formulas. Think of computing the one-hundredth term of a sequence for which you only have a recursive formula and the value of the first term. You would have to compute the value of every term between the first and the hundredth!

Thus, you should learn the direct counterparts for some common recursive formulas.

1) Linear (or arithmetic) sequence
Remember, in a linear sequence, the difference between successive terms is always the same.

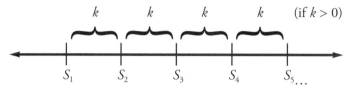

A linear sequence can be defined either with $S_n = kn + x$ or with $S_n = S_{n-1} + k$ and $S_1 = k + x$.

If k is the constant difference between successive terms, and x is some other constant, then we have the following definitions:

Direct formula	Recursive formula
$S_n = kn + x$	$S_n = S_{n-1} + k$
	$S_1 = k + x$

> The first two terms of sequence S_n are $S_1 = 8$ and $S_2 = 6$. If the difference between each successive term is constant, what is the recursive rule for this sequence? What is the fiftieth term of this sequence?

We compute the difference between the first two terms (keep track of the order) as -2. Thus, we know that $S_n = S_{n-1} + (-2) = S_{n-1} - 2$. All we need to do is specify any other term, such as $S_1 = 8$ or $S_2 = 6$, and we have a complete recursive definition for the sequence. However, to find the fiftieth term of the sequence, we should find the direct formula. We already know that $k = -2$, the constant difference between terms. Since $S_1 = 8$, we can solve for x as follows: $S_1 = k + x$
$$8 = (-2) + x$$
$$10 = x$$

Now, we know that we can write the direct formula: $S_n = kn + x = -2n + 10$. It is often worth checking that your direct formula matches the terms you already know. For instance, $S_2 = -2(2) + 10 = 6$, which matches the value given for the second term. Finally, we can write the fiftieth term of the sequence: $S_{50} = -2(50) + 10 = -90$.

2) Exponential (or geometric) sequence
In an exponential sequence, the *ratio* between successive terms is always the same. This is because each term is equal to the previous term *times* a constant.

If k is the constant ratio between successive terms, and x is some other constant, then we have the following definitions:

<u>Direct formula</u>

$S_n = xk^n$

<u>Recursive formula</u>

$S_n = kS_{n-1}$

$S_1 = xk$

In sequence C_n, we are given that $C_3 = 12$ and $C_5 = 3$. If each term is equal to the previous term times a constant number, and if all the terms in the sequence are positive, what is the recursive rule for this sequence? What is the value of C_{10}?

As we figure out this sequence, we have to be careful, since we are not given successive terms. We know that $C_3 = 12$ and $C_5 = 3$. We also know that the sequence is geometric, since each term equals the previous term times a constant. Thus, we can set up the general recursive formula for this type of sequence: $C_n = kC_{n-1}$

We can rewrite this formula in two specific ways:

$C_4 = kC_3$

$C_5 = kC_4$

Combining these equations, we get the following: $C_5 = kC_4 = k(kC_3) = k^2C_3$

Now, we can solve for k:

$3 = k^2(12)$

$3/12 = k^2$

$1/4 = k^2$

$1/2 = k$ or $-1/2 = k$

However, the requirement that all terms be positive eliminates the possibility that $k = -1/2$, since a negative k would force every other term to be negative. Thus, we know that $k = 1/2$. (In general, k does not have to be greater than 1. It can be less than 1 or even less than 0, in other problems.) Now we can rewrite the general recursive formula: $C_n = (1/2)C_{n-1}$

Together with the value of any term, we have a complete definition of the sequence. However, to compute the tenth term, we should find the direct formula for the sequence, so we need the value of x, the other constant in the formula. Use the general form of the direct rule:

$C_n = xk^n = x(1/2)^n$

$C_3 = x(1/2)^3$

$12 = x(1/8)$

$96 = x$ Notice that x is not itself C_1. $C_1 = xk = (96)(1/2) = 48$.

Plug in $n = 10$ to find C_{10}:

$C_{10} = xk^{10} = 96(1/2)^{10}$

$C_{10} = (3)(2^5)/(2^{10})$

$C_{10} = (3)/(2^5) = 3/32$

You can also set up a table of values and extract the pattern. The safer and more general method, however, is to solve for the unknown constants k and x and write the direct formula for the term you want.

> An exponential sequence can be defined either with $S_n = xk^n$ or $S_n = kS_{n-1}$ and $S_1 = xk$.

Advanced Function Types

EXPONENTIAL GROWTH

Although not as common as linear growth, **exponential growth** also appears occasionally on GMAT problems. In exponential growth, a quantity is multiplied by the same constant each period of time (rather than adding the same constant, as in linear growth). Any exponential growth can be written as $y(t) = y_0 \cdot k^t$, in which y represents the quantity as a function of time t, y_0 is the value of the quantity at time $t = 0$, and k represents the constant multiplier for one period. Commonly, exponential growth multipliers take the form of percentage multipliers. For instance, for a quantity that increases by 7% each period, $k = 1.07$.

> Any quantity that doubles in a set amount of time is growing exponentially.

Notice the similarity between this formula for exponential growth and the formula for an exponential sequence ($S_n = xk^n$), where x and k are constants). The difference is that with $y(t) = y_0 \cdot k^t$, the variable t can take on non-integer values. In a sequence, n must be an integer, typically 1 or greater.

> A quantity increases in a manner such that the ratio of its values in any two consecutive years is constant. If the quantity doubles every 6 years, by what factor does it increase in two years?

There are a couple of phrases to notice in this problem. First, "...such that the ratio of its values in any two consecutive years is constant" implies exponential growth, so the quantity can be represented by the function $y(t) = y_0 \cdot k^t$. Second, "by what factor" refers to a multiplier of the original quantity.

The value of the quantity at time zero ($t = 0$) is y_0. Because the quantity doubles every 6 years, its value at time $t = 6$ years must be $2y_0$. Therefore:

$$2y_0 = y_0(k^6) \qquad\qquad 2 = k^6 \text{ (notice that } y_0 \text{ cancels out)} \qquad \sqrt[6]{2} = k$$

The factor by which the quantity increases in two years ($t = 2$) is $k^2 = \sqrt[6]{2^2} = \sqrt[3]{2}$.

For more on Exponential Growth, see the "Rates & Work" chapter of the Manhattan GMAT *Word Translations* Strategy Guide.

SYMMETRY

Some difficult GMAT function questions revolve around "symmetry," or the property that two seemingly different inputs to the function always yield the same output.

> For which of the following functions does $f(x) = f\left(\dfrac{1}{x}\right)$, given that $x \neq -2, -1, 0,$ or 1?

(A) $f(x) = \left|\dfrac{x+1}{x}\right|$ (C) $f(x) = \left|\dfrac{x-1}{x}\right|$ (E) $f(x) = \left|\dfrac{x+1}{x+2}\right|$

(B) $f(x) = \left|\dfrac{x+1}{x-1}\right|$ (D) $f(x) = \left|\dfrac{x}{x+1}\right|$

*Manhattan*GMAT*Prep
the new standard

There are two primary ways that we can set about solving this problem. First, we could substitute $\dfrac{1}{x}$ in for x in each of the functions and simplify, to see which of the functions yields the same result. Alternatively, we could pick a number for x and see which of the functions produces an equal output for both x and $\dfrac{1}{x}$. In most cases, the latter strategy will probably be easier. For example, we could choose $x = 3$:

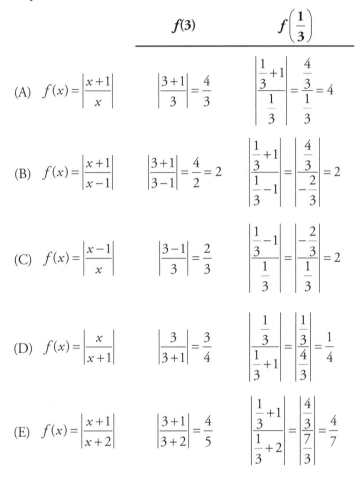

For "Symmetry" function problems, you can either pick numbers and test the functions, or solve algebraically.

Only (B) returns the same result for 3 and $\dfrac{1}{3}$, so it is the correct answer. We can also prove that (B) is the correct answer algebraically:

$$f(x) = \left| \frac{x+1}{x-1} \right|$$

$$f\left(\frac{1}{x}\right) = \left| \frac{\frac{1}{x}+1}{\frac{1}{x}-1} \right| = \left| \frac{\frac{x+1}{x}}{\frac{1-x}{x}} \right| = \left| \frac{x+1}{1-x} \right| = \left| \frac{x+1}{-(1-x)} \right| = \left| \frac{x+1}{x-1} \right|$$

PROPERTIES

Other advanced function problems on the GMAT test whether certain functions follow certain properties of mathematics. For example:

For which of the following functions does $f(x - y)$ NOT EQUAL $f(x) - f(y)$?

For which of the following functions does $f(a(b + c)) = f(ab) + f(ac)$?

For all of these questions a quick, effective approach is simply to pick numbers and see which function gives the desired result.

> For optimization problems involving linear functions, check all endpoints to determine which combination of endpoints gives the optimal value.

Optimization Problems

Some GMAT problems will present you with functions and ask you to find the maximum or minimum value of those functions. Broadly speaking, you will be called upon to maximize or minimize only two types of functions: linear and quadratic.

LINEAR FUNCTIONS

As you will recall, a linear function has (or can be reduced to) the form $f(x) = mx + b$, where m and b are constants. For instance, $y = 3x - 4$ is a linear function, as are and $y + 6 = 7(x - 4)$. As their name implies, linear functions have straight-line graphs, which either rise continuously or fall continuously as x increases. As a result, the extremes (the maximum and the minimum) of linear functions occur **at the boundaries: at the smallest possible x and the largest possible x, as given in the problem.**

> If $f(x) = 3 - 4x$ and $g(z) = 5 + 2z$, and x and z are each between 0 and 10, inclusive, what is the maximum value for $f(x) + g(z)$?

First, we need to find the maximum values of EACH of f and g within their given ranges.

For the function f: $f(0) = 3 - 4(0) = 3$, while $f(10) = 3 - 4(10) = -37$. The maximum value of $f(x)$ is 3, and the minimum value of $f(x)$ is -37.

For the function g: $g(0) = 5 + 0 = 5$; $g(10) = 5 + 20 = 25$. The maximum value of $g(z)$ is 25, and the minimum value of $g(z)$ is 5.

Therefore, the maximum value of $f(x) + g(z)$ occurs when $x = 0$ and $z = 10$, yielding a value of $3 + 25 = 28$.

QUADRATIC FUNCTIONS

Unlike linear functions, quadratic functions do not grow continuously or decline continuously. Rather, they form parabolas. A parabola has either a peak (a maximum value) or a valley (a minimum value). This "peak point" or "valley point" is what you need to find.

ManhattanGMAT Prep
the new standard

Let us consider the simplest quadratic function: $f(x) = x^2$. Squares are almost always positive. The only square that is not positive is 0^2, which equals 0. So this function has its lowest value (0) when x itself is also equal to 0. The parabola which represents $y = f(x) = x^2$ opens upward and has a "valley" or minimum point at (0, 0).

Every other quadratic function is just a variation of $f(x) = x^2$. The minimum or maximum of every other quadratic function depends on the property that the smallest square is 0, which is the square of 0.

Note: Not to scale.

1. $f(x) = x^2 + 1$ is shifted upward by 1 unit. The minimum value of the function is 1, and that minimum occurs when $x = 0$.

> Pay attention to how changes to a quadratic function change its graph--and the position of its extreme point.

2. $f(x) = x^2 - 3$ is shifted downward by 3 units. The minimum value of the function is -3, and that minimum occurs when $x = 0$.

3. $f(x) = 2x^2 + 1$ is shifted upward by 1 unit <u>and</u> squeezed (it has steeper slopes than $x^2 + 1$). However, the factor of 2 does not affect the position of the minimum point. Just as with the function $x^2 + 1$, the minimum value of the function is 1, and that minimum occurs when $x = 0$.

4. $f(x) = -x^2$ is flipped over: the parabola now looks like a peak, not a valley. However, the position of the extreme point is still (0, 0)—in other words, $x = 0$ and $y = 0$. The only difference is that this point is now a maximum, not a minimum. We see that the sign of the squared term determines whether the extreme point is a minimum (positive sign) or a maximum (negative sign).

5. $f(x) = 2 + (x + 3)^2$ looks more complicated. First, we should focus on the squared expression: $(x + 3)^2$ must be at least 0, so the minimum occurs when $(x + 3)^2$ is exactly equal to 0. This occurs when $x = -3$, not when $x = 0$. At $x = -3$, $f(x) = 2 + [(-3) + 3]^2 = 2 + 0 = 2$. Any other value of x will result in a larger value for y. On a coordinate plane, this parabola is shifted 2 units up and 3 units left, but it still opens upward.

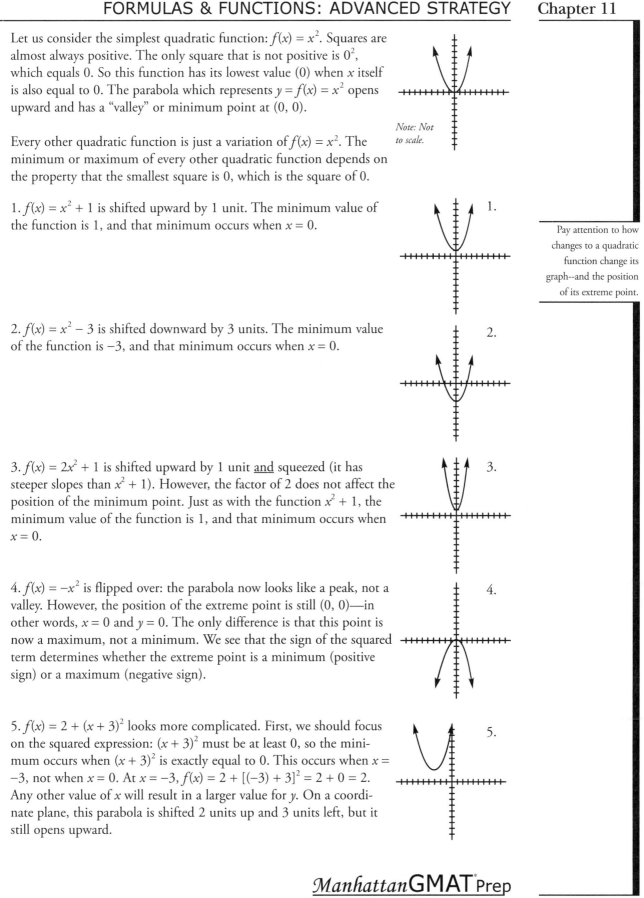

The key to deciphering the function is to **make the squared expression equal to 0**. Whatever value of x makes the squared expression equal to 0 is the value of x that minimizes or maximizes the function. The resulting value of the function is the minimum or the maximum of the function. (The function has a minimum if other values of the square make the function bigger, whereas the function has a maximum if other values of the square make the function smaller.)

Consider the quadratic function $f(x) = 7 - (x + 1)^2$.

(a) Does this function have a minimum value or a maximum value?
(b) At what value of x does this minimum or maximum occur?
(c) What is the minimum or maximum value?

To solve optimization problems involving perfect square quadratics, simply set the perfect square term equal to zero.

Answer (a): The perfect square is subtracted. This is the same as having a negative coefficient (specifically, -1). The term $-(x+1)^2$ has either a negative value or a value of zero, so the function will have a <u>maximum</u> value when the squared term is zero.

Answer (b): The maximum occurs when the perfect square itself is zero. This will happen when $x + 1 = 0$, or $x = -1$.

Answer (c): Since the maximum occurs when the perfect square is zero, the value of the maximum is $7 - 0^2 = 7$.

Problem Set (Advanced)

For problem #1, use the following sequence: $A_n = 3 - 8n$

1.   What is the equivalent recursive definition for this sequence?

For problems #2–4, use the following sequence: $S_n = 3S_{n-1}$, for all integer n $\geq$ 2

2.   If $S_1 = 15$, what is $S_4 - S_2$?

3.   If $S_3 = 540$, what is S_1?

4.   What is the equivalent explicit rule for this sequence, if $S_1 = 1$?

5.   A sequence is defined as follows: $a_1 = 1$, and $a_n = na_{n-1}$ for all integer $n \geq 2$. Write an explicit formula for a_n in terms of n.

6.   If $f(x) = (x - 1)^2$, what is the value of $f(x - 1)$?
      (A) $x^2 + 2x + 1$ (B) $x^2 - 4x + 2$ (C) $x^2 - 4x + 4$ (D) $x^2 + 4x + 4$

7.   If $f(x) = 3x - 1$ and $g(x) = x^2$, what is $g(f(3x + 1))$?

8.   If $k(x) = x + 1$, and $j(x) = 2x - 4$, for what value will $k(x) = j(k(x))$?

9.   A certain kudzu plant was 11 feet long on the day it was planted, and the length grows by a constant amount every day (including the first day it was planted). If this plant grew 40% between the fourth day after it was planted and the tenth day after it was planted, how many feet per day does it grow?

10.   A strain of bacteria multiplies such that the ratio of its population in any two consecutive minutes is constant. If the bacteria grows from a population of 5 million to a population of 40 million in one hour, by what factor does the population increase every 10 minutes?

11.   For which of the following functions does $f(x) = f(2 - x)$?
      (A) $f(x) = x + 2$ (B) $f(x) = 2x - x^2$ (C) $f(x) = 2 - x$
      (D) $f(x) = (2 - x)^2$ (E) $f(x) = x^2$

12.   For which of the following functions does $f(cd) = f(c)f(d)$?
      (A) $f(x) = x + 2$ (B) $f(x) = 2x - x^2$ (C) $f(x) = 2 - x$
      (D) $f(x) = (2 - x)^2$ (E) $f(x) = x^2$

13.   If $f(x) = 7 - 5x$ and $g(y) = 5 + 3y$, and x and y are between -5 and 5, inclusive, what is the maximum value for $f(x) - g(y)$?

14.   If $f(x) = 24 + (2x + 1)^2$, what is the minimum value for $f(x)$, and what is the value of x at which this minimum occurs?

1. $A_n = A_{n-1} - 8$; $A_1 = -5$: Because each term in A is 8 fewer than the previous term, the sequence is linear, and the recursive formula definition is simply $A_n = A_{n-1} - 8$. You can supply the value of any term in the sequence to complete the definition (it does not have to be A_1).

2. **360:** One way to solve this problem is to simply keep multiplying by 3 to get the next term. $S_1 = 15$, so $S_2 = 15(3) = 45$, $S_3 = 45(3) = 135$, and $S_4 = 135(3) = 405$. Therefore $S_4 - S_2 = 405 - 45 = 360$.

You could also leave the calculations until the end:
$$S_2 = 3(15) \qquad S_3 = 3^2(15) \qquad S_4 = 3^3(15)$$
$$S_4 - S_2 = 3^3(15) - 3(15) = 3(15)(3^2 - 1) =$$
$$3(15)(8) = 360$$

3. **60:** One way to solve this problem is to work backward: simply keep DIVIDING by 3 to get PRIOR terms in the sequence. $S_3 = 540$, so $S_2 = \dfrac{540}{3} = 180$, and $S_1 = \dfrac{180}{3} = 60$. Alternatively, write $S_1 = x$, $S_2 = 3x$, $S_3 = 3(3x) = 9x = 540$, so $x = 60 = S_1$.

4. 3^{n-1}: Write out the first few terms of the sequence, starting with $S_1 = 1$. Since $S_n = 3S_{n-1}$, we generate the next term by multiplying by 3: $S_2 = 3S_1 = 3(1) = 3$. $S_3 = 3S_2 = 3(3) = 9$. $S_4 = 3S_3 = 3(9) = 27$. You should now notice that you are creating the powers of 3. The only remaining question is how exactly those powers match up to the position n. Working backwards, we see that the *fourth* term $S_4 = 27$, which is 3^3 (three *cubed*, or three to the *third* power). Likewise, the *third* term $S_3 = 9$, which is 3^2 (three *squared*, or three to the *second* power). The pattern is that the power of three has an exponent that is *one less* than the position of the term. We can write this generalization as 3^{n-1}.

5. $a_n = n!$:
$$a_1 = 1$$
$$a_2 = 1 \times 2 = 2$$
$$a_3 = (1 \times 2) \times 3 = 6$$
$$a_4 = (1 \times 2 \times 3) \times 4 = 24$$

Each of these terms adds the latest n to the end of a long string of multiplication, starting from 1 and counting up to n. This is the definition of a factorial, so the explicit formula is $a_n = n!$.

6. **(C):** Plug the variable expression $x - 1$ into the rule for the function $f(x)$.
$$f(x - 1) = [(x - 1) - 1]^2$$
$$= (x - 2)^2$$
$$= x^2 - 4x + 4$$

Alternately, you might solve this problem as a VIC (see the VIC chapter in this book) by picking a number for x and evaluating $f(x)$ for $x - 1$. Then, you would evaluate each answer choice to find the one that matches your target value.

7. $81x^2 + 36x + 4$: First, find the output value of the inner function:
$$f(3x + 1) = 3(3x + 1) - 1$$
$$= 9x + 3 - 1 = 9x + 2$$

Then, find $g(9x + 2)$: $(9x + 2)^2 = (9x + 2)(9x + 2) = 81x^2 + 36x + 4$.

8. $x = 3$: First, simplify $j(k(x))$.
$$j(k(x)) = j(x + 1) = 2(x + 1) - 4 = 2x - 2$$

To find the values for which $k(x) = j(k(x))$, set the functions equal to each other.
$$x + 1 = 2x - 2$$
$$x = 3$$

9. **1 foot per day:** This is a linear growth problem, so we should use the equation $y = mx + b$. The original length of the plant is given, so $b = 11$. Since the growth rate m is unknown, the growth function can be written as $y = mx + 11$. The length of the plant after the fourth day is $y = 4m + 11$ and after the tenth day, $y = 10m + 11$. We know that the length of the plant on the tenth day is 40% greater than the length on the fourth day, so now we can solve for m:

$$10m + 11 = (4m + 11) + 0.40(4m + 11)$$
$$10m + 11 = 1.4(4m + 11)$$
$$10m + 11 = 5.6m + 15.4$$
$$4.4m = 4.4$$
$$m = 1$$

10. $\sqrt{2}$: This is an exponential growth problem, so we should use the equation $y(t) = y_0 \cdot k^t$. In one hour (60 minutes), the population grows by a factor of $\dfrac{40,000,000}{5,000,000} = 8$, which also equals k^{60}. Thus, in one minute, the population grows by a factor of $k = \sqrt[60]{8} = \sqrt[60]{2^3} = \sqrt[20]{2}$. The question asks what factor the population will grow by in 10 minutes, so we simply take this factor to the tenth power: $k^{10} = \left(\sqrt[20]{2}\right)^{10} = \sqrt{2}$. Alternatively, you could notice that $8 = 2^3$, so an hour equals 3 periods of doubling. In other words, the population doubles every 20 minutes. In 10 minutes, therefore, the population increases by a factor of $\sqrt{2}$. (In this way, two periods of 10 minutes lead to an increase by a factor of $\sqrt{2} \times \sqrt{2} = 2$.)

11. **(B)** $f(x) = 2x - x^2$: This is a "symmetry function" type of problem. Generally the easiest way to solve these kinds of problems is to pick numbers and plug them into each function to determine which answer gives the desired result. For example, you could pick $x = 4$:

	$f(4)$	$f(2-4)$
(A) $f(x) = x + 2$	$4 + 2 = 6$	$(2 - 4) + 2 = 0$
(B) $f(x) = 2x - x^2$	$2(4) - 4^2 = -8$	$2(2 - 4) - (2 - 4)^2 =$ $-4 - 4 = -8$
(C) $f(x) = 2 - x$	$2 - 4 = -2$	$2 - (2 - 4) = 4$
(D) $f(x) = (2 - x)^2$	$(2 - 4)^2 = 4$	$[2 - (2 - 4)]^2 =$ $4^2 = 16$
(E) $f(x) = x^2$	$4^2 = 16$	$(2 - 4)^2 = 4$

*Manhattan*GMAT*Prep
the new standard

12. **(E)** $f(x) = x^2$: This is a "properties of math" function problem. Often the easiest way to solve these kinds of problems is to pick numbers and plug them into each function to determine which answer gives the desired result. For example, you could pick $c = 3$ and $d = 4$:

	$f(3 \times 4)$	$f(3)f(4)$
(A) $f(x) = x + 2$	$3 \times 4 + 2 = 14$	$(3 + 2)(4 + 2) =$ $5 \times 6 = 30$
(B) $f(x) = 2x - x^2$	$2(12) - 12^2 = -120$	$(6 - 3^2)(8 - 4^2) =$ $(-3)(-8) = 24$
(C) $f(x) = 2 - x$	$2 - (3 \times 4) = -10$	$(2 - 3)(2 - 4) =$ $(-1)(-2) = 2$
(D) $f(x) = (2 - x)^2$	$(2 - 3 \times 4)^2 = (-10)^2$ $= 100$	$(2 - 3)^2(2 - 4)^2 =$ $(-1)^2(-2)^2 = 4$
(E) $f(x) = x^2$	$(3 \times 4)^2 = 144$	$3^2 \times 4^2 = 144$

Upon reflection, this should make sense algebraically: $(c \times d)^2 = c^2 \times d^2$.

13. **42:** We need to find the maximum value for $f(x) - g(y)$. This can be found by taking the LARGEST value of $f(x)$, and subtracting the SMALLEST value of $g(y)$:

$f(-5) = 7 - 5(-5) = 7 + 25 = 32$, and $f(5) = 7 - 5(5) = 7 - 25 = -18$, so $f(-5)$ returns the highest value.

$g(-5) = 5 + 3(-5) = 5 - 15 = -10$, and $g(5) = 5 + 3(5) = 5 + 15 = 20$, so g(-5) returns the lowest value.

The maximum value for $f(x) - g(y) = 32 - (-10) = 42$.

14. **$f(x) = 24; x = -\dfrac{1}{2}$** : If $f(x) = 24 + (2x + 1)^2$, then $f(x)$ will be minimized when the squared term equals zero:

$$(2x + 1)^2 = 0$$
$$2x + 1 = 0$$
$$x = -\frac{1}{2}$$
$$f(-\frac{1}{2}) = 24 + \left[2\left(-\frac{1}{2}\right) + 1\right]^2 = 24 + 0^2 = 24$$

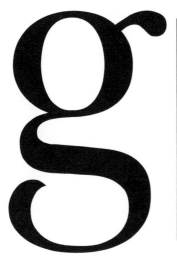

Chapter 12
of
EQUATIONS, INEQUALITIES, & VICs

INEQUALITIES:
ADVANCED

In This Chapter . . .

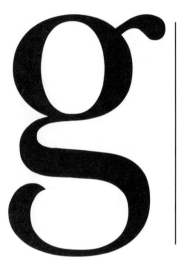

- Working with Advanced Inequalities
- Reciprocals of Inequalities
- Squaring Inequalities
- A Challenging Problem

Working with Advanced Inequalities

In the Inequalities chapter in Part 1, we mentioned that when you multiply or divide an inequality by a negative number, the inequality sign flips. We also mentioned the corollary: you cannot multiply or divide an inequality by a variable unless you know the sign of the variable. The reason is that you would not know whether to flip the inequality sign. Consider this example:

$$\text{Given that } \frac{x}{y} < 1, \text{ is } x < y?$$

The answer would seem obvious because when we multiply both sides of the inequality by y, we get $x < y$. However, because we do not know whether y is positive or negative, we are NOT ALLOWED to multiply both sides of the equation by y without considering two separate cases.

If y is positive, then the solution to the inequality is in fact $x < y$. However, if y is negative, we are multiplying an inequality by a negative number; thus, the sign flips and yields the solution $x > y$. Here are two scenarios with real numbers to prove this:

CASE	VALUES	CONDITION	RESULT
$y > 0$	$x = 3$ $y = 4$	$\dfrac{3}{4} < 1$	$3 < 4$, so $x < y$
$y < 0$	$x = -1$ $y = -2$	$\dfrac{-1}{-2} < 1$	$-1 > -2$, so $x > y$

Therefore, we cannot answer this question with the given information without knowing the sign of y.

This example might be recast in a Data Sufficiency problem. For example:

Is $x < y$?

(1) $\dfrac{x}{y} < 1$

(2) $y > 0$

The trap answer to this problem is A: Statement 1 alone is sufficient. However, once you recognize that you also need to know the sign of y, you will realize the correct answer is **(C)**: Both statements TOGETHER are sufficient, but neither statement alone is sufficient.

This sort of Data Sufficiency problem is common enough at the hardest levels of the GMAT that you should be wary of answer choices A or B on problems involving inequalities and variables. In such cases, you might also need the condition from the other Statement to answer the question. A seemingly inconsequential statement, such as "x is positive" or "a is negative," is often crucial on inequality problems.

If you must multiply or divide a statement by a variable before you know its sign, set up two cases —the positive and negative case—and solve each one separately to arrive at two possible scenarios.

Reciprocals of Inequalities

Taking reciprocals of inequalities is similar to multiplying/dividing by negative numbers. You need to consider the positive/negative cases of the variables involved. The general rule is that **if $x < y$, then:**

- $\dfrac{1}{x} > \dfrac{1}{y}$ **when x and y are positive.** Flip the inequality. If $3 < 5$, then $\dfrac{1}{3} > \dfrac{1}{5}$.

- $\dfrac{1}{x} > \dfrac{1}{y}$ **when x and y are negative.** Flip the inequality. If $-4 < -2$, then $\dfrac{1}{-4} > \dfrac{1}{-2}$.

- $\dfrac{1}{x} < \dfrac{1}{y}$ **when x is negative and y is positive.** Do NOT flip the inequality.

If $-6 < 7$, then $\dfrac{1}{-6} < \dfrac{1}{7}$. The left side is negative, while the right side is positive.

- **If we do not know the sign of x or y, we cannot take reciprocals.**

In summary, if you know the signs of the variables, you should flip the inequality UNLESS x and y have different signs.

> Given that $ab < 0$ and $a > b$, which of the following must be true?
>
>   I. $a > 0$
>   II. $b > 0$
>
>   III. $\dfrac{1}{a} > \dfrac{1}{b}$
>
> (A) I only
> (B) II only
> (C) I and III only
> (D) II and III only
> (E) I, II and III

We know from the problem stem that $ab < 0$ and $a > b$. This tells us that a and b have different signs, so a must be positive and b must be negative. Therefore I is true, while II is not true.

We also know from the discussion on reciprocals that if $a > b$, then $\dfrac{1}{a} < \dfrac{1}{b}$ (the inequality is flipped) UNLESS a and b have different signs, in which case $\dfrac{1}{a} > \dfrac{1}{b}$. Since a and b have different signs here, $\dfrac{1}{a} > \dfrac{1}{b}$. Therefore the correct answer is **(C)**.

Squaring Inequalities

As with reciprocals, you cannot square both sides of an inequality unless you know the signs of both sides of the inequality. However, the rules for squaring inequalities are somewhat different from those for reciprocating inequalities.

- **If both sides are known to be negative, then flip the inequality sign when you square.** For instance, if $x < -3$, then the left side must be negative. Since both sides are negative, you can square both sides and reverse the inequality sign: $x^2 > 9$. However, if you are given an inequality such as $x > -3$, then you cannot square both sides, because it is unclear whether the left side is positive or negative. If x is negative, then $x^2 < 9$, but if x is positive, then x^2 could be either greater than 9 or less than 9.

- **If both sides are known to be positive, then do not flip the inequality sign when you square.** For instance, if $x > 3$, then the left side must be positive; since both sides are positive, you can square both sides to yield $x^2 > 9$. If you are given an inequality such as $x < 3$, however, then you cannot square both sides, because it is unclear whether the left side is positive or negative. If x is positive, then $x^2 < 9$, but if x is negative, then x^2 could be either greater than 9 or less than 9.

- **If one side is positive and one side is negative, then you cannot square.** For example, if we know that $x < y$, x is negative, and y is positive, we cannot make any determination about x^2 vs. y^2. If, for example, $x = -2$ and $y = 2$, then $x^2 = y^2$. If $x = -2$ and $y = 3$, then $x^2 < y^2$. If $x = -2$ and $y = 1$, then $x^2 > y^2$. It should be noted that if one side of the inequality is negative and the other side is positive, the squaring is probably not warranted—some other technique is likely needed to solve the problem.

- **If the signs are unclear, then you cannot square.** Put simply, you would not know whether to flip the sign of the inequality once you have squared it.

> Is $x^2 > y^2$?
> (1) $x > y$
> (2) $x > 0$

In this problem, we need to know whether $x^2 > y^2$. Statement 1 is insufficient, because we do not know whether x and y are positive or negative numbers. For example, if $x = 5$ and $y = 4$, then $x^2 > y^2$. However, if $x = -4$ and $y = -5$, then $x > y$ but $x^2 < y^2$.

Statement 2 does not tell us anything about y, so it too is insufficient.

Combined, we know that x is positive and larger than y. This is still insufficient, because y could be a negative number of larger magnitude than x. For example, if $x = 3$ and $y = 2$, then $x^2 > y^2$, but if $x = 3$ and $y = -4$, then $x^2 < y^2$. Therefore, the correct answer is (**E**).

You can only square inequalities when both sides have the same sign—and the sign must be known to be positive or negative.

A Challenging Problem

Consider the following example, a challenging problem that incorporates several inequality techniques.

Is $a > 0$?

(1) $a^3 - a < 0$
(2) $1 - a^2 > 0$

First, we have inequalities with zero on one side of the inequality. Thus, we should consider using positive/negative analysis. We can factor Statement 1 as follows:

$$a^3 - a < 0$$
$$a(a^2 - 1) < 0$$

How is this helpful? Now we have an inequality in the form $xy < 0$. When you see an inequality of this type, you should think "x and y have different signs." Therefore a and $a^2 - 1$ have different signs, so we have two scenarios to consider:

a	$a^2 - 1$
$+$	$-$
$-$	$+$

In the first scenario, a is positive, and $a^2 - 1$ is negative. Therefore $a > 0$ and $a^2 - 1 < 0$. If $a^2 - 1 < 0$, then $a^2 < 1$ and $|a| < 1$. Thus:

$$0 < a \text{ and } -1 < a < 1$$

In this scenario, a must be both positive AND between -1 and 1. We can combine the two inequalities to $0 < a < 1$.

In the second scenario, $a < 0$ and $a^2 - 1 > 0$. If $a^2 - 1 > 0$, then $a^2 > 1$ and $|a| > 1$. Thus:

$$a < 0 \text{ and } (a < -1 \text{ or } a > 1).$$

In this scenario, a must be both negative AND either less than -1 or greater than 1. It is impossible for a to be both negative and greater than 1, so we can focus only on the second possibility: a is both negative and less than -1. The condition $a < -1$ is more restrictive than the condition $a < 0$, so we can combine the two inequalities into $a < -1$.

Taking the two results together, we see that Statement 1 rephrases to: $a < -1$ OR $0 < a < 1$. On the number line, these conditions look like the following:

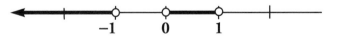

Because we cannot tell whether a is positive, Statement 1 is insufficient.

You could also use test numbers with $a^3 - a < 0$ to identify the regions that work, but you would have to test numbers in 4 regions:

> A difficult inequality problem, especially in data sufficiency, may require you to combine multiple techniques from this chapter, in order to find the solution.

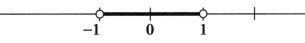

$a < -1$	$-1 < a < 0$	$0 < a < 1$	$1 < a$
$a = -2$	$a = -0.5$	$a = 0.5$	$a = 2$
$(-2)^3 - (-2) < 0$?	$(-0.5)^3 - (-0.5) < 0$?	$(0.5)^3 - (0.5) < 0$?	$(2)^3 - (2) < 0$?
YES	NO	YES	NO

Statement 2 tells us that $1 - a^2 > 0$. Therefore, $a^2 < 1$. This tells us that $|a| < 1$, so $-1 < a < 1$. On the number line, this condition looks like the following:

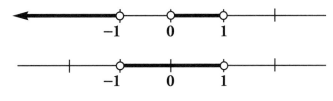

This does not tells us whether a is positive, so Statement 2 is insufficient. When we combine the two Statements, we find that a must be positive.

Statement 1 tells us that: $a < -1$ OR $0 < a < 1$
Statement 2 tells us that: $-1 < a < 1$

In order for both of these statements to be true, a must be between 0 and 1. Therefore, Statements 1 and 2 combined are SUFFICIENT, and the correct answer is **(C)**.

Notice that we could also solve this problem by using the number lines we drew for each statement. Since both statements need to be true, we would take only the regions where the two drawings overlap:

The region where the two number lines overlap is $0 < a < 1$, so we know a is positive:

As an aside, recall that when we factored Statement 1, the result was:

$a(a^2 - 1) < 0$

Also recall that Statement 2 was:

$1 - a^2 > 0$

Notice that Statement 2 is the negative of the second factored term. In other words, $(1 - a^2) = -(a^2 - 1)$. Thus if we multiply Statement 2 by -1, we get:

$a^2 - 1 < 0$

We could now interpret the problem as follows:

Statement (1) tells me that either a or $a^2 - 1$ is negative, but not both.
Statement (2) tells me that $a^2 - 1$ is negative. Therefore, a must be positive, and the correct answer is **(C)**.

*Manhattan*GMAT®Prep
the new standard

Problem Set (Advanced)

1.   If $x > y$, $x < 6$, and $y > -3$, what is the largest prime number that could be equal to $x + y$?

2.   If $2x > 3y$ and $4y > 5z$, and z is positive, which of the following must be true?
        (A) $x < y < z$ (B) $2x < 3y < 5$ (C) $2x > 4y > 5z$ (D) $8x > 12y > 15z$

3.   Given that a, b, c, and d are integers, and that $a < b$, $d > c$, $c > b$, and $d - a = 3$, which of the following must be true?
        (A) $b = 2$ (B) $d - b = 3$ (C) $c - a = 1$ (D) $c - b = 1$ (E) $a + b = c + d$

4.   If $TG > 0$ and G is negative, which of the following must be positive?
        (A) $T + G$ (B) $2T + G$ (C) $T - G$ (D) $G - T$ (E) $-G - T$

5.   A cyclist travels the length of a bike path that is 225 miles long, rounded to the nearest mile. If the trip took him 5 hours, rounded to the nearest hour, then his average speed **must** be between:

        (A) 38 and 50 miles per hour   (B) 40 and 50 miles per hour
        (C) 40 and 51 miles per hour   (D) 41 and 50 miles per hour
        (E) 41 and 51 miles per hour

6.   If a and b are integers and $-4 \leq a \leq 3$ and $-4 \leq b \leq 5$, what is the maximum possible value for ab?

7.   If $a = 4 - (2b - 1)^2$, at what value of b is a maximized?

8.   Is $mn > -12$?
        (1) $m > -3$
        (2) $n > -4$

9.   Is $x^3 > x^2$?
        (1) $x > 0$
        (2) $x^2 > x$

10.   If $\dfrac{4}{x} < \dfrac{1}{3}$, what is the possible range of values for x?

11.   If $\dfrac{4}{x} < -\dfrac{1}{3}$, what is the possible range of values for x?

12.   If $x \neq 0$, is $\dfrac{x^2 + 1}{x} > y$?

        (1) $x = y$
        (2) $y > 0$

13.   Is $x < y$?

(1) $\dfrac{1}{x} < \dfrac{1}{y}$

(2) $\dfrac{x}{y} < 0$

14.   Is $x^2 > y^2$?
(1) $x < y$
(2) $y < 0$

15.   Is $w - x < y - z$?
(1) $y > w$
(2) $z < x$

1. **11:** Simplify the inequalities, so that all the inequality symbols point in the same direction. Then, line up the inequalities as shown. Finally, combine the inequalities.

$$y < x$$
$$x < 6 \qquad \rightarrow \qquad -3 < y < x < 6$$
$$-3 < y$$

There is no integer constraint.
x could be 5.6, and y could be 5.4.
In this case, $x + y = 11$.

2. **(D):** First, multiply the first and second inequalities by appropriate factors so that the inequalities have the common term $12y$.

$$4(2x > 3y) \rightarrow 8x > \mathbf{12y}$$
$$3(4y > 5z) \rightarrow \mathbf{12y} > 15z$$

Simplify the inequalities, so that all the inequality symbols point in the same direction. Then, line up the inequalities and combine.

$$0 < 15z$$
$$15z < 12y \qquad \rightarrow \qquad 0 < 15z < 12y < 8x$$
$$12y < 8x$$

3. **(D):** Simplify the inequalities, so that all the inequality symbols point in the same direction. Then, line up the inequalities as shown. Finally, combine the inequalities.

$$a < b$$
$$b < c \qquad \rightarrow \qquad a < b < c < d$$
$$c < d$$

Since we know that $d - a = 3$, we know that the variables a, b, c, and d are consecutive integers, in ascending order. We can prove this by picking numbers for d and a. For example, assume $d = 8$ and $a = 5$. Since b and c must be between 5 and 8 and must be integers, the only possible values are 6 and 7. Moreover, b must be smaller than c, so b must be 6 and c must be 7. Therefore, $c - b = 1$.

4. **(E):** If G is negative, T must also be negative. You can generate counter-examples to eliminate each incorrect answer choice.

(A) $T + G \quad \rightarrow \quad -3 + (-4) = -7 \qquad$ Incorrect
(B) $2T + G \quad \rightarrow \quad 2(-1) + (-6) = -8 \qquad$ Incorrect
(C) $T - G \quad \rightarrow \quad -5 - (-3) = -2 \qquad$ Incorrect
(D) $G - T \quad \rightarrow \quad -7 - (-4) = -3 \qquad$ Incorrect

It is impossible to generate an example in which the value of (E) is negative. $-G$ will always be a positive number, since G is negative. Subtracting a negative number (T) from a positive number ($-G$) will always yield a positive number.

5. **(C) 40 and 51 miles per hour:** If the cyclist rode 225 miles, rounded to the nearest mile, and took 5 hours, rounded to the nearest hour, he traveled between 224.5 miles and 225.5 miles, and took between 4.5 and 5.5 hours. The maximum speed can be obtained by dividing the largest possible number of miles (225.5) by the SMALLEST (4.5) number of hours. Similarly, the minimum speed can be obtained by dividing the smallest number of miles (224.5) by the LARGEST number of hours (5.5):

$$\text{Maximum speed} = \frac{225.5}{4.5} = \frac{225.5(2)}{4.5(2)} = \frac{451}{9} = 50\frac{1}{9} \text{ miles per hour}$$

$$\text{Minimum speed} = \frac{224.5}{5.5} = \frac{224.5(2)}{5.5(2)} = \frac{449}{11} = 40\frac{9}{11} \text{ miles per hour}$$

Therefore, the cyclist's speed must be between 40 and 51 miles per hour.

6. **16:** In order to maximize ab, we need to test the endpoints of the ranges for a and b:

If $a = -4$ and $b = -4$, $ab = 16$.
If $a = -4$ and $b = 5$, $ab = -20$.
If $a = 3$ and $b = -4$, $ab = -12$.
If $a = 3$ and $b = 5$, $ab = 15$.

Thus the maximum value for ab is 16. Notice that this maximum occurs when a and b are both negative in this case.

7. $b = \dfrac{1}{2}$: The value of a will be maximized when the quadratic expression $(2b - 1)^2$ is minimized—in other words, when it is set equal to 0. This means that $(2b - 1) = 0$:

$$2b = 1$$

$$b = \frac{1}{2}$$

8. **(E):** Combining the two statements, it is tempting to conclude that mn must either be positive or a negative number larger than -12. However, because either variable could be positive or negative, it is possible to end up with a negative number less than -12. For example, m could equal -1 and n could equal 50. In that case, $mn = -50$, which is less than -12. Therefore, the two statements combined are INSUFFICIENT. The correct answer is (E).

9. **(C):** We can factor the question as follows:

$$x^3 > x^2?$$
$$x^3 - x^2 > 0?$$
$$x^2(x - 1) > 0?$$

Both terms must be positive or negative, because we have an inequality in the form $xy > 0$. x^2 can never be negative, so we just need to know that both $x^2 > 0$ (meaning x is non-zero) and $x > 1$. Since every number greater than 1 is non-zero, we can rephrase the question simply to:

$$x > 1?$$

Statement (1) tells us x is positive. INSUFFICIENT.
Statement (2) tells is that $x^2 > x$, so $x < 0$ OR $x > 1$. INSUFFICIENT.

Combining the two statements, we know that $x > 1$. SUFFICIENT.

10. **$x < 0$ OR $x > 12$:** For this type of problem, we have to consider two possibilities: x could be positive or negative. When we multiply the inequality by x, we will need to flip the sign when x is negative, but not flip the sign when x is positive:

Case 1: $x > 0$	**Case 2: $x < 0$**
$\dfrac{4}{x} < \dfrac{1}{3}$	$\dfrac{4}{x} < \dfrac{1}{3}$
$12 < x$	$12 > x$

For Case 1, x must be positive AND greater than 12. Thus, $x > 12$.
For Case 2, x must be negative AND less than 12. Thus, $x < 0$.

Combined, $x < 0$ OR $x > 12$.

11. **$-12 < x < 0$:** For this type of problem, we have to consider two possibilities: x could be positive or negative. When we multiply the inequality by x, we will need to flip the sign when x is negative, but not flip the sign when x is positive. However, notice that x CANNOT be positive: the left-hand side of the inequality is less than $-\dfrac{1}{3}$, which means $\dfrac{4}{x}$ must be negative. Therefore x must be negative:

Case 1: $x > 0$	**Case 2: $x < 0$**
Not possible	$\dfrac{4}{x} < -\dfrac{1}{3}$
	$12 > -x$
	$-12 < x$

Case 1 is not possible.
For Case 2, x must be negative AND greater than -12. Thus, $-12 < x < 0$.

12. **(C):** It is tempting to use Statement (1) and multiply the question by x:

Is $x^2 + 1 > xy$?   Is $x^2 + 1 > x^2$?

This would seem to be sufficient, because we could then cancel out the x^2 terms and the question could be rephrased to:

Is $1 > 0$?

However, if we multiply through by x, we are assuming that x is positive. If x were negative, we would need to flip the sign when we multiply by x, producing 2 cases:

If $x > 0$:	**If $x < 0$:**
Is $x^2 + 1 > x^2$?	Is $x^2 + 1 < x^2$?

The answer to the first question is "yes", and the answer to the second question is "no." Therefore

Statement (1) is INSUFFICIENT.
Statement (2) on its own is INSUFFICIENT, because it tells us nothing about x.

Therefore we must evaluate Statements (1) and (2) combined. Statement (2) tells us that y is positive (thus, x is positive). Therefore, we can multiply the question by x without flipping the sign, and get:

$$\text{Is } x^2 + 1 > xy? \qquad\qquad \text{Is } x^2 + 1 > x^2? \qquad\qquad \text{Is } 1 > 0?$$

The answer is yes, so the correct answer is **(C)**.

13. **(C):** The meaning of Statement (1) depends on the signs of x and y. If x and y are either both positive or both negative, then you can take reciprocals of both sides, yielding $x > y$. However, this statement could also be true if x is negative and y is positive; in that case, $x < y$. INSUFFICIENT.

Statement (2) tells us that the quotient of x and y is negative. In that case, x and y have different signs: one is positive and the other is negative. However, this does not tell you which one is positive and which one is negative. INSUFFICIENT.

Combining the two statements, if we know that the reciprocal of x is less than that of y, and that x and y have opposite signs, then x must be negative and y must be positive, so $x < y$. SUFFICIENT. The correct answer is **(C)**.

14. **(C):** Statement (1) is insufficient, because we do not know whether x and y are positive or negative numbers. For example, if $x = 3$ and $y = 4$, then $x^2 < y^2$. However, if $x = -4$ and $y = -3$, then $x < y$ but $x^2 > y^2$.

Statement (2) does not tell us anything about x, so it too is insufficient.

Combined, we know that y is negative and x is smaller than y. Therefore x is also negative, and x is a negative number with a larger absolute value than y. If $|x| > |y|$, then we know that $x^2 > y^2$. SUFFICIENT. The correct answer is **(C)**.

15. **(C):** This question can be solved by adding inequalities together. The first step is to rephrase the question so that all of the terms have positive coefficients:

$$
\begin{array}{l}
\text{Is } w - x < y - z? \\
\underline{\quad\quad +x \quad\quad\quad +x \quad\quad} \\
\text{Is } w \quad\quad < y - z + x?
\end{array}
$$

$$
\begin{array}{l}
\text{Is } w \quad\quad < y - z + x? \\
\underline{\quad\quad +z \quad\quad +z \quad\quad} \\
\textbf{Is } w + z < y + x?
\end{array}
$$

Now we can arrange the statements so that their inequality signs line up, and add them together:

$$
\begin{array}{ll}
\text{Statement (1):} & w \quad\ < y \\
\text{Statement (2):} & \underline{+\ (\quad z < \quad x\ )} \\
\text{Combined:} & \boldsymbol{w + z < y + x}
\end{array}
$$

Therefore Statements (1) and (2) together are SUFFICIENT.

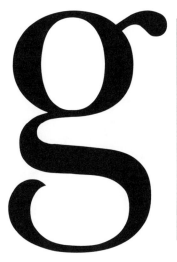

Chapter 13
of

EQUATIONS, INEQUALITIES, & VICs

ADDITIONAL
VICS PRACTICE

Problem Set (Advanced)

1. If $b = \dfrac{3a - 6}{4}$, then what is a?

   (A) $\dfrac{12b}{5}$ (B) $\dfrac{4b - 6}{3}$ (C) $\dfrac{3b + 6}{4}$ (D) $\dfrac{4b + 6}{3}$ (E) $3b + 6$

2. What number is x percent of y percent of z, in terms of x, y, and z?

   (A) $\dfrac{xyz}{10,000}$ (B) $\dfrac{xy + xz}{10,000}$ (C) $\dfrac{xyz + 100xz}{10,000}$ (D) $\dfrac{xyz}{100}$ (E) $\dfrac{xy + xz}{100}$

3. x is what percent greater than y, in terms of x and y?

   (A) $100\left(\dfrac{x + y}{y}\right)$ (B) $100\left(\dfrac{y}{x + y}\right)$ (C) $100\left(\dfrac{x - y}{y}\right)$

   (D) $100\left(\dfrac{y}{x - y}\right)$ (E) $\dfrac{100x - y}{y}$

4. x is what percent of y percent of z, in terms of x, y and z?

   (A) $\dfrac{100xy}{z}$ (B) $\dfrac{100yz}{x}$ (C) $\dfrac{100y}{xz}$ (D) $\dfrac{10,000x}{yz}$ (E) $\dfrac{10,000yz}{x}$

5. If $a = 20bc$, then a is what percent of b?

   (A) $20c$ (B) $2,000c$ (C) $\dfrac{c}{20}$ (D) $\dfrac{c}{2,000}$ (E) $c + 20$

6. If a, b, and c are greater than 0 and a is twice as large as b percent of c, then in terms of b and c, what is a percent of c?

   (A) $\dfrac{2bc}{100}$ (B) $\dfrac{2bc^2}{1,000}$ (C) $\dfrac{bc^2}{5,000}$ (D) $\dfrac{b^2c}{5,000}$ (E) $\dfrac{5,000b}{c^2}$

7. X percent of Y percent of Z is decreased by Y percent. What is the result?

   (A) $\dfrac{100XYZ - XY^2Z}{1,000,000}$ (B) $\dfrac{XZ - Y}{100}$ (C) $\dfrac{XZ - Y}{10,000}$

   (D) $\dfrac{XYZ - 2Y}{100}$ (E) $\dfrac{XYZ - 2Y}{10,000}$

8. Two wooden boards have the same area. One of the boards is square and the other is rectangular. If the square board has a perimeter of p meters and the rectangular board has a width of w meters, what is the length of the rectangular board, in terms of p and w?

   (A) $\dfrac{p^2}{w}$ (B) $\dfrac{p^2}{4w}$ (C) $\dfrac{p^2}{16w}$ (D) $\dfrac{p^2w}{4}$ (E) $\dfrac{p^2w}{16}$

9.   Bradley owns b video game cartridges. If Bradley's total is one-third the total owned by Andrew and four times the total owned by Charlie, how many video game cartirdges do the three of them own altogether, in terms of b?

(A) $\dfrac{16}{3}b$ (B) $\dfrac{17}{4}b$ (C) $\dfrac{13}{4}b$ (D) $\dfrac{19}{12}b$ (E) $\dfrac{7}{12}b$

10.   Linda and Angela contract to paint a neighbor's house. Even though Linda spends 50% more time painting the house than Angela, each receives a payment of m dollars when the work is completed. If Angela decides to pay Linda n dollars so that they would have received the same compensation per hour worked, what is n in terms of m?

(A) $\dfrac{1}{2}m$ (B) $\dfrac{1}{3}m$ (C) $\dfrac{1}{4}m$ (D) $\dfrac{1}{5}m$ (E) $\dfrac{1}{6}m$

11.   A park ranger travels from his base to a camp site via truck at r miles per hour. Upon arriving, he collects a snowmobile and uses it to return to his base. If the camp site is d miles from the park ranger's base and the entire trip took t hours to complete, what was his speed on the snowmobile, in terms of t, d and r?

(A) $tr - d$ (B) $td - r$ (C) $\dfrac{dr}{rt - d}$ (D) $\dfrac{drt}{dt - r}$ (E) $\dfrac{td - r}{d}$

*Manhattan*GMAT Prep
the new standard

1. **(D):** Using the **Direct Algebra** strategy, we solve for a and see which answer choice matches our result:

$$b = \frac{3a-6}{4} \qquad\qquad 4b+6 = 3a$$

$$4b = 3a - 6 \qquad\qquad \frac{4b+6}{3} = a$$

2. **(A):** Using the principles laid out for Percent VICs in this chapter, this problem can be solved relatively easily using the **Direct Algebra** approach: "x percent of…" translates to "$\frac{x}{100} \times \dots$", and "$y$ percent of z"

translates to "$\frac{y}{100} \times z$." Therefore "x percent of y percent of z" translates to $\frac{x}{100} \times \frac{y}{100} \times z = \frac{xyz}{10,000}$.

3. **(C):** This problem can be solved by using the **Direct Algebra** approach. "x is what percent greater than y" can be solved by creating an intermediate variable, such as w, to represent the percent of y that x is greater than, and then solve for w. Recall that "percent greater than y" means "y, plus a percent of y":

$$x = y + \frac{w}{100} \times y \qquad\qquad x - y = \frac{wy}{100}$$

$$x - y = \left(\frac{w}{100}\right) y \qquad\qquad 100\left(\frac{x-y}{y}\right) = w$$

Alternatively, you could use the **Hybrid Method**. Say $x = 50$ and $y = 40$. Then x is 25 percent greater than y. How do we use 50 and 40 to arrive at 25? Simply subtract 40 from 50, divide $(50 - 40) = 10$ by 40,

then multiply by 100: $100\left(\dfrac{50-40}{40}\right) = 100\left(\dfrac{x-y}{y}\right)$.

4. **(D):** This problem can be solved by using the **Direct Algebra** approach. "x is what percent of y percent of z" can be broken down into two components. First, "y percent of z" translates to "$\dfrac{y}{100} \times z$." Second, "x is what percent of y percent of z" can be solved by creating an intermediate variable, such as w, to represent the percent of "y percent of z" that x equals, and then solve for that variable:

$$x = \frac{w}{100} \times \frac{y}{100} \times z \qquad x = \frac{w\left(\frac{yz}{100}\right)}{100} \qquad \frac{100x}{\frac{yz}{100}} = w \qquad \frac{10,000x}{yz} = w$$

5. **(B):** Let us use the **Pick Numbers and Calculate a Target** approach. Select values for a, b, and c that make the equation $a = 20bc$ true, such as $a = 120$, $b = 2$, and $c = 3$. Since $120 \div 2 = 60$, a is 6,000% of b. Test each answer choice to find the one that yields the Target value of 6,000.

(A) $20c = 20 \times 3 = 60$ Incorrect

(B) $2,000c = 2,000 \times 3 = 6,000$ CORRECT

(C) $\dfrac{c}{20} = \dfrac{3}{20}$ Incorrect

(D) $\dfrac{c}{2,000} = \dfrac{3}{2,000}$ Incorrect

(E) $c + 20 = 3 + 20 = 23$ Incorrect

6. **(C):** Let us use the **Pick Numbers and Calculate a Target** approach. Select values for a, b, and c such that a is twice the size of b percent of c. For example, $a = 80$, $b = 25$, and $c = 160$. Since 80% of 160 = 128, we should test each answer choice to find the one that yields the Target value of 128.

(A) $\dfrac{2bc}{100} = \dfrac{2(25)(160)}{100} = \dfrac{50(160)}{100} = 80$ Incorrect

(B) $\dfrac{2bc^2}{1,000} = \dfrac{2(25)(160)^2}{1,000} = \dfrac{160^2}{2} = 12,800$ Incorrect

(C) $\dfrac{bc^2}{5,000} = \dfrac{25(160)^2}{5,000} = \dfrac{(160)^2}{200} = 128$ CORRECT

(D) $\dfrac{b^2c}{5,000} = \dfrac{(25)^2 160}{5,000} = \dfrac{25(160)}{200} = 20$ Incorrect

(E) $\dfrac{5,000b}{c^2} = \dfrac{5,000(25)}{(160)^2} = \dfrac{50(25)}{16^2} = \dfrac{625}{128}$ Incorrect

7. **(A):** Let us use the **Pick Numbers and Calculate a Target** approach. First, assign numbers to represent X, Y, and Z. We should pick numbers that translate easily into percents, such as those in the table to the right, because solving this problem will require heavy computation.

variable	number
X	10
Y	50
Z	200

        Y% of Z = 50% of 200 = 100
        X% of Y% of Z = 10% of 100 = 10
        Decreasing this result by Y%, or by 50%, yields 5.

Next, test each answer choice to find the one that yields the Target value of 5:

(A) $\dfrac{100XYZ - XY^2Z}{1,000,000} = \dfrac{100(10)(50)(200) - (10)(2500)(200)}{1,000,000} = 5$ CORRECT

(B) $\dfrac{XZ - Y}{100} = \dfrac{(10)(200) - 50}{100} = 19$ Incorrect

(C) $\dfrac{XZ - Y}{10,000} = \dfrac{(10)(200) - 50}{10,000} = 0.19$ Incorrect

(D) $\dfrac{XYZ - 2Y}{100} = \dfrac{(10)(50)(200) - 2(50)}{100} = 999$ Incorrect

(E) $\dfrac{XYZ - 2Y}{10,000} = \dfrac{(10)(50)(200) - 2(50)}{10,000} = 9.99$ Incorrect

*Manhattan*GMAT*Prep
the new standard

Note that if you find the calculations taking too long to complete, you could stop and choose **(A)**, because it matched our target. This ignores the possibility that **(A)** matched the target by coincidence and some other answer choice is correct. However, it may be better to take a good chance on **(A)** and conserve time than to spent a large amount of time to prove that **(A)** is correct. This strategy would not be as effective if the correct answer were not one of the first answer choices evaluated.

8. **(C):** Let us solve this problem using a **Pick Numbers and Calculate a Target** approach. First, draw a diagram to represent the problem. Then assign numbers to represent p and w. We should try to pick numbers that will result in the length being an integer, if possible.

variable	number
p	24
w	2

If the perimeter of the square is 24, then each side of the square must equal 6. Therefore the area of the square will be $6^2 = 36$. If the width of the rectangle is 2, then the length of the rectangle (shown as L) must be 18 so that the rectangle also has an area of 36.

Test each answer choice to find the one that yields the Target value of 18:

(A) $\dfrac{p^2}{w} = \dfrac{24^2}{2} = 288$ Incorrect

(B) $\dfrac{p^2}{4w} = \dfrac{24^2}{4(2)} = 72$ Incorrect

(C) $\dfrac{p^2}{16w} = \dfrac{24^2}{16(2)} = 18$ CORRECT

(D) $\dfrac{p^2 w}{4} = \dfrac{24^2(2)}{4} = 288$ Incorrect

(E) $\dfrac{p^2 w}{16} = \dfrac{24^2(2)}{16} = 72$ Incorrect

9. **(B):** Let us solve this problem using a **Pick Numbers and Calculate a Target** approach. Imagine that Bradley owns 12 video game cartridges. Then Andrew owns 36 video game cartridges and Charlie owns 3 video game cartridges. In total, the three boys own $12 + 36 + 3 = 51$ video game cartridges. Therefore we should test each answer choice to find the one that yields the Target value of 51:

(A) $\dfrac{16}{3}b = \dfrac{16}{3}(12) = 64$ Incorrect

(B) $\dfrac{17}{4}b = \dfrac{17}{4}(12) = 51$ CORRECT

(C) $\dfrac{13}{4}b = \dfrac{13}{4}(12) = 39$ Incorrect

You should take a glance at the relationships before picking numbers. For example, since Bradley owns 4 times as many video game cartridges as Charlie, Bradley's total should be a number divisible by 4 (such as 12).

(D) $\dfrac{19}{12}b = \dfrac{19}{12}(12) = 19$ Incorrect

(E) $\dfrac{7}{12}b = \dfrac{7}{12}(12) = 7$ Incorrect

*Manhattan*GMAT*Prep
the new standard

10. (D): For this problem, we can use the **Hybrid Method**. The problem contains two variables and an implicit equation, so we have to pick a value for one of the variables and solve for the other variable. We will also invent a variable to represent the number of hours Linda and Angela worked.

Let us assume m, the original payment in dollars to both Linda and Angela, equals $50. If Angela worked x hours, then Linda worked $1.5x$ hours. Therefore, pick $x = 2$ (to produce integers for both Angela's hours and Linda's hours). Angela has to make a payment to Linda of n dollars so that both Linda and Angela earn the same hourly wage.

Linda's hourly wage is given by: $\dfrac{50+n}{3} = \dfrac{m+n}{3}$

Angela's hourly wage is given by: $\dfrac{50-n}{2} = \dfrac{m-n}{2}$

Therefore, we have:

$$\dfrac{m+n}{3} = \dfrac{m-n}{2} \qquad\qquad 5n = m$$
$$2m + 2n = 3m - 3n \qquad\qquad n = \dfrac{1}{5}m$$

11. (C): This is a Rates & Work problem that can be solved using an RTD Chart. We will use the **Direct Algebra** method to think through the problem. Additionally, we will invent a variable, q, to represent the park ranger's speed on the snowmobile:

(units)	Rate (miles/hour)	×	Time (hours)	=	Distance (miles)
Truck	r	×	$\dfrac{d}{r}$	=	d
Snowmobile	q	×	$\dfrac{d}{q}$	=	d
Total		×	t	=	$2d$

Since Rate × Time = Distance, Time = Distance ÷ Rate. Therefore we know that the time that the park ranger spent in the truck was $\dfrac{d}{r}$ hours and the time he spent driving the snowmobile was $\dfrac{d}{q}$ hours.

Furthermore, those times have to sum to the total time for the trip, so $\dfrac{d}{r} + \dfrac{d}{q} = t$. We can now solve for q:

$$\dfrac{d}{r} + \dfrac{d}{q} = t \qquad dq + dr = rqt \qquad q(d - rt) = -dr \qquad q = \dfrac{-dr}{d - rt} = \dfrac{dr}{rt - d}$$

For more on solving Rates & Work problems, see the "Rates & Work" chapter of the Manhattan GMAT *Word Translations* Strategy Guide.

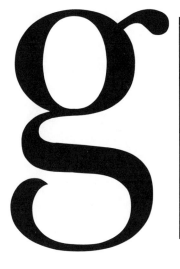

Chapter 14
of
EQUATIONS, INEQUALITIES, & VICs

OFFICIAL GUIDE
PROBLEM SETS:
PART II

In This Chapter . . .

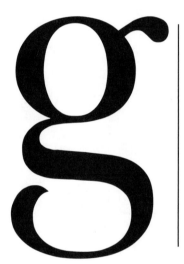

- Equations, Inequalities, & VICs Problem Solving List
  from *The Official Guides:* PART II
- Equations, Inequalities, & VICs Data Sufficiency List
  from *The Official Guides:* PART II

Practicing with REAL GMAT Problems

Now that you have completed Part II of *EQUATIONS, INEQUALITIES & VICs* it is time to test your skills on problems that have actually appeared on real GMAT exams over the past several years.

The problem sets that follow are composed of questions from three books published by the Graduate Management Admission Council® (the organization that develops the official GMAT exam):

The Official Guide for GMAT Review, 12th Edition
The Official Guide for GMAT Quantitative Review
The Official Guide for GMAT Quantitative Review, 2nd Edition
Note: The two editions of the Quant Review book largely overlap. Use one OR the other.

These books contain quantitative questions that have appeared on past official GMAT exams. (The questions contained therein are the property of The Graduate Management Admission Council, which is not affiliated in any way with Manhattan GMAT.)

Although the questions in the Official Guides have been "retired" (they will not appear on future official GMAT exams), they are great practice questions.

In order to help you practice effectively, we have categorized every problem in The Official Guides by topic and subtopic. On the following pages, you will find two categorized lists:

(1) **Problem Solving:** Lists MORE DIFFICULT Problem Solving Equations, Inequalities & VIC questions contained in *The Official Guides* and categorizes them by subtopic.

(2) **Data Sufficiency:** Lists MORE DIFFICULT Data Sufficiency Equations, Inequalities & VIC questions contained in *The Official Guides* and categorizes them by subtopic.

Each book in Manhattan GMAT's 8-book strategy series contains its own *Official Guide* lists that pertain to the specific topic of that particular book. If you complete all the practice problems contained on the *Official Guide* lists in each of the 8 Manhattan GMAT strategy books, you will have completed every single question published in *The Official Guides*.

Problem Solving: Part II

from *The Official Guide for GMAT Review, 12th Edition* (pages 20–23 & 152–185), *The Official Guide for GMAT Quantitative Review* (pages 62–85), and *The Official Guide for GMAT Quantitative Review, 2nd Edition* (pages 62–86). <u>Note</u>: The two editions of the Quant Review book largely overlap. Use one OR the other.

Solve each of the following problems in a notebook, making sure to demonstrate how you arrived at each answer by showing all of your work and computations. If you get stuck on a problem, look back at the EQUATIONS, INEQUALITIES, and VICs strategies and content contained in this guide.

<u>Note</u>: Problem numbers preceded by "D" refer to questions in the Diagnostic Test chapter of *The Official Guide for GMAT Review, 12th edition* (pages 20–23).

ADVANCED SET – EQUATIONS, INEQUALITIES, & VICs

This set picks up from where the General Set in Part I left off.

Basic Equations
> *12th Edition*: 196, 218
> *Quantitative Review*: 155, 173

Equations with Exponents
> *12th Edition*: 150, 172
> *Quantitative Review*: 153, 166 OR *2nd Edition*: 166

Quadratic Equations
> *12th Edition*: 215, 222
> *Quantitative Review*: 121 OR *2nd Edition*: 121

Formulas & Functions
> *12th Edition*: 146, 171, 228
> *QR 2nd Edition*: 67, 131, 158

Inequalities
> *12th Edition*: 161, 173
> *QR 2nd Edition*: 156

VICs
> *12th Edition*: 163, 165, 202, 204, 208, 212, 213, 227
> *Quantitative Review*: 118, 124, 128, 133, 146, 171, 172
> OR *2nd Edition*: 118, 124, 128, 133, 171, 172

CHALLENGE SHORT SET – EQUATIONS, INEQUALITIES, & VICs

This set covers Equations, Inequalities, and VIC problems from each of the content areas, including both easier and harder problems, but with a focus on harder problems. The Challenge Short Set duplicates problems from the General Set (in Part I) and the Advanced Set above.

> *12th Edition*: 34, 38, 41, 58, 68, 89, 122, 130, 144, 146, 163, 173, 188, 196, 204, 208, 212, 213, 215, 222, 228, D16, D24
> *Quantitative Review*: 52, 83, 85, 92, 104, 106, 107, 153, 155, 173
> OR *2nd Edition*: 41, 54, 85, 92, 103, 104, 106, 107, 131, 156

Data Sufficiency: Part II

from *The Official Guide for GMAT Review, 12th Edition* (pages 24–26 & 272–288), *The Official Guide for GMAT Quantitative Review* (pages 149–157), and *The Official Guide for GMAT Quantitative Review, 2nd Edition* (pages 152–163). <u>Note</u>: The two editions of the Quant Review book largely overlap. Use one OR the other.

Solve each of the following problems in a notebook, making sure to demonstrate how you arrived at each answer by showing all of your work and computations. If you get stuck on a problem, look back at the EQUATIONS, INEQUALITIES, AND VICs strategies and content contained in this guide. Practice REPHRASING both the questions and the statements by manipulating equations and inequalities. The majority of data sufficiency problems can be rephrased; however, if you have difficulty rephrasing a problem, try testing numbers to solve it. It is especially important that you familiarize yourself with the directions for data sufficiency problems, and that you memorize the 5 fixed answer choices that accompany all data sufficiency problems.

<u>Note</u>: Problem numbers preceded by "D" refer to questions in the Diagnostic Test chapter of *The Official Guide for GMAT Review, 12th edition* (pages 24–26).

ADVANCED SET – EQUATIONS, INEQUALITIES, & VICs
This set picks up from where the General Set in Part I left off.

Basic Equations
12th Edition: 95, 125, 150, 168, D37
Quantitative Review: 92, 102, 103, 118 OR *2nd Edition*: 106, 124

Equations with Exponents
12th Edition: 165
Quantitative Review: 105, 115 OR *2nd Edition*: 109, 121

Quadratic Equations
12th Edition: 158
Quantitative Review: 79, 80 OR *2nd Edition*: 83

Formulas & Functions
12th Edition: 115
QR 2nd Edition: 107, 111

Inequalities
12th Edition: 97, 153, 162, D38
Quantitative Review: 66, 67, 85, 114 OR *2nd Edition*: 68, 69, 89, 120

CHALLENGE SHORT SET – EQUATIONS, INEQUALITIES, & VICs
This set covers Equations, Inequalities, and VIC problems from each of the content areas, including both easier and harder problems, but with a focus on harder problems. The Challenge Short Set duplicates problems from the General Set (in Part I) and the Advanced Set above.
12th Edition: 26, 30, 38, 45, 80, 97, 115, 125, 154, 156, 158, 162, 168, D30, D33
Quantitative Review: 85, 115 OR *2nd Edition*: 89, 121

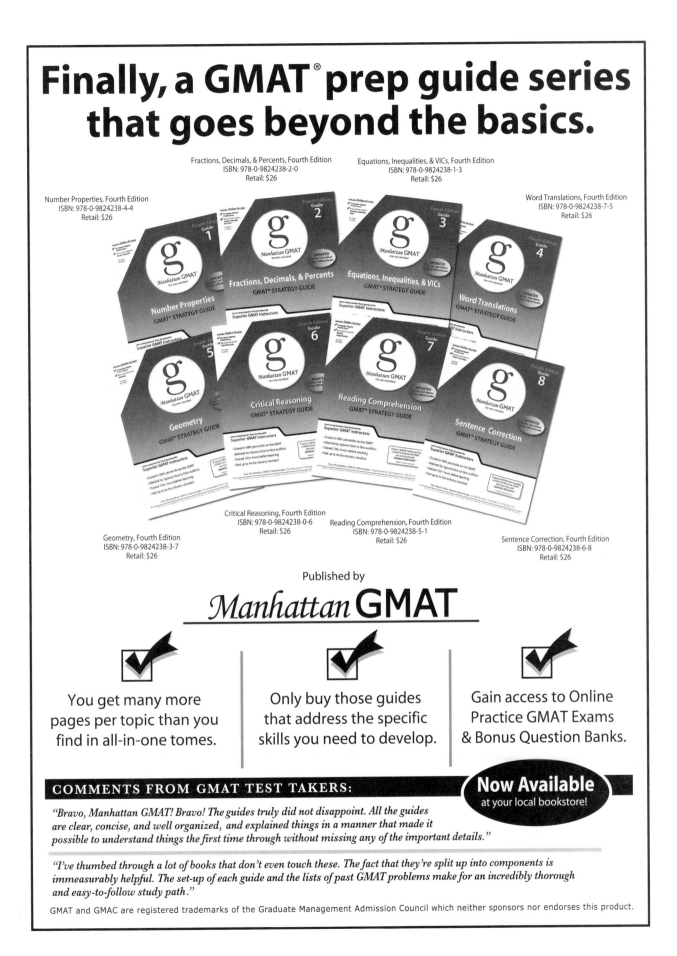